Reviews for

REACHING BEYOND THE VEIL

"At a time when ghostly encounters are sadly and most often depicted as, and defined by, people covered in electronic gadgets shouting the names of the deceased into moldy basements and dark attics, April Slaughter restores heart, humility and sincerity to one of humanity's oldest, yet often misunderstood dialogues. In fostering a sense of obligation and sympathy between the living and the dead, April shows what this relationship once was and can continue to be: a loving exchange between neighbors and kin."
Ari Berk, Ph.D.
Professor of Folklore and Mythology
Central Michigan University
Author of *The Undertaken Trilogy*

"I have been the subject of many interviews over the last ten years. I can honestly say that my interview with April was the most interesting I've ever had. She was full of ideas and insights that I had not considered. At one point, I felt like I was interviewing her. This book is a must read, even for people who have read many other books in the field of afterlife research."
Dr. Allan L. Botkin
Clinical Psychologist & author of *Induced After Death*
Communication: A New Therapy for Healing Grief and Trauma

"April Slaughter presents a compelling personal journey into the heart of communicating with the dead, and gives a refreshing and honest assessment of an often controversial field. Anyone who has ever reached out to loved ones in the afterlife will find this book insightful and inspiring."
Rosemary Ellen Guiley
Co-author, *Talking to the Dead*

"April Slaughter takes a controversial subject and provides the reader with an intimate yet well-researched perspective. Even if one disbelieves in afterlife communication, Slaughter shows the human face and living relevancy of communicating with the departed."
Deonna Kelli Sayed
Author of *Paranormal Obsession: America's Fascination with Ghosts & Hauntings, Spooks & Spirits.*

"Death ends a life, not a relationship."
Mitch Albom

REACHING

BEYOND the

VEIL

unlocking the mystery of modern spirit communication

april slaughter

For my beautiful daughters Jordyn and Madison.
I believe in miracles because you are living proof that they exist.

For my grandfather Reed,
who is always with me in thought *and* spirit.

Original Cover Artwork Designed by
© Copyright 2013 by Scott Alan Roberts and April Slaughter

Edited by Jill Hand

Ouija® is a registered trademark of Hasbro

Names throughout this book have been changed to protect the identities of the individuals involved. The details of their stories have not been altered.

This Book is Published by:
Whitechapel Press
A Division of Apartment #42 Productions
Decatur, Illinois / 1-888-GHOSTLY
Visit us on the internet at www.whitechapelpress.com

ISBN: 1-892523-82-5

Printed in the United States of America

ACKNOWLEDGEMENTS

This project has been one especially close to my heart, as have the various individuals who have shared their time, knowledge and patience in order to help make it possible. I extend my gratitude to anyone with whom I have had lengthy discussions about the afterlife, whether or not we agreed by conversation's end. I thank my colleagues and critics alike for continually encouraging me to push further, dig deeper, and to never stop questioning.

I am deeply indebted to Troy Taylor for not only taking on the project, but for his belief in my ability to do the job well. I owe thanks to both he and Rosemary Ellen Guiley for their contributions to the paranormal field, as their prolific research and works have played an integral role in my supernatural studies long before I ever met them.

Had it not been for the unwavering support and unflappable honesty of my friend and fellow writer John Melchior, I may never have discovered the courage to commit my thoughts to paper the first time, let alone on the occasions that have since materialized.

I owe thanks to the following individuals for lending me a friendly ear whenever I needed it, and for sharing their insights on a subject so near and dear to my heart: Thomas Young, James Boley, Allen Slaughter, James and Mary Hampton, Amber Barnes, Adam and Gabriela Norton, Jerry Bowers, Paulina Cassidy, Deonna Kelli, Michael Kravchuk, Marc Magsaysay, Angelka Rogers, Rob Graves, Anthony Armstrong, David C. Cowan, C.J. Sellers, Scotty Roberts, Steve Mangin, Dr. Ciarán O'Keeffe, Orrin Taylor, and the countless others who deserve thanks whom I have neglected to list by name.

I thank Dr. Allan L. Botkin for introducing me to his work with Induced After-Death Communication, and for his willingness to spend time with me to discuss it. I also extend my gratitude to his colleague Dr. Graham Maxey for assisting me in my desire to personally experience the "other side" through IADC. The resulting knowledge and reinforced connection to those I love is a gift I cannot adequately measure.

There are numerous individuals whom I encounter at various times that I cannot see, but who are no less important in my progression with this research and to whom I owe my gratitude. The so-called "dead" are with me often. Without their help, I could not have held onto and strengthened my faith in the immortality of the spirit.

TABLE OF CONTENTS

FOREWORD

Here Mr. Splitfoot, do as I do...
Knock, knock.

Knock, knock.

Believe it or not, that's how it started – at least during our modern era.

Since the beginning of recorded time, man has claimed to be able to communicate with the spirit world. However, it would not be until the heyday of the Spiritualist movement in the mid-nineteenth century that he would begin claiming to do so as an everyday occurrence. The teenage Fox sisters of Hydesville, New York, founders of the movement, established a way to communicate with a ghost. They knocked, asked the ghost to reply and it did! Thus, history was made. By using a series of knocks and raps that signified "yes" or "no," and then creating a code corresponding to the letters of the alphabet, contact with the spirit world was established.

For many bereaved people, Spiritualism was a godsend. The early and middle nineteenth century was a time of short life expectancy and high child mortality rates. Two out of every ten babies did not live to see their first birthday. It was not unusual for mothers to die during childbirth. Simply surviving to adulthood was considered an achievement and even then, a great many people did not live beyond their forties. Medical treatment was limited, painful and often deadly. There were no therapists to help the grieving deal with death. Whether they knew it or not, the mediums of the Spiritualist movement were suddenly placed in the role of grief counselors. Spirit contact meant comfort to the grieving and attending séances became more than mere entertainment; for many, it became a necessity.

Séances, or "sittings," were usually held in the home of a medium or of one of the sitters. To begin, the lights were turned down low or extinguished altogether. The participants were generally seated in a circle around a round table, with men and women alternating. They either linked hands with the persons on either side of them, placing their clasped hands on the table, or they placed their hands flat on the table, fingers lightly touching those of their neighbors.

There were a number of unwritten rules for séances. Usually, no more than two or three were held in a week, lasting for no more than two hours unless the spirits asked for more time. Sitters were warned not to touch the medium or any of the manifested spirits, unless the spirits touched them first. Such interference, they were told, could cause the medium to snap out of her trance, resulting in the risk of her becoming physically ill, insane, or possibly even dying!

A variety of phenomena were reported at the séances. Sitters often recognized the arrival of the spirits by a rush of cold air in the room, followed by rapping and tapping, knocking and perhaps strange lights, sounds and voices. The phenomena would often intensify as the evening progressed. Simple noises and floating lights were often followed by elaborate messages from the departed, usually coming directly through the medium.

In the 1850s, it was not unusual to be invited to someone's house for tea and "table tipping," one of the most popular home circle entertainments of the day. Those who participated in this type of séance were asked to place their hands on a table and then wait until it moved, turned or tilted of its own volition. Not unlike spirit rapping, messages "came through" as the table tilted in a pre-established code that corresponded to the letters of the alphabet. Séance participants would often speak directly to the table, asking it questions that it answered through turns and tips.

Although table tipping dated back to the days of ancient Rome, it became enormously popular in America during the early days of Spiritualism. Spiritualists explained that the process worked through a form of psychic energy that emitted from each and every object in the world. Mediums were supposed to be especially sensitive to this energy.

While Spiritualists embraced table tipping, others found it sinful and potentially dangerous. In churches, ministers railed against it as demonic, while a number of physicians warned it could cause participants to go insane.

Another popular form of mediumship was a phenomenon known as "automatic writing." As interest in Spiritualism grew and more people became involved in it, the tiresome and time-consuming method of knocking and rapping fell out of fashion as mediums began to produce written messages from the spirit world. All that was needed was a pencil

8

and some sheets of paper. The medium would go into a trance, take up the pencil and begin to write. It was believed by some that the spirits literally manipulated the pencil in the hands of the medium, causing her to scrawl out text in handwriting that was markedly different than her own. Other mediums claimed to receive psychic messages from the spirits, which they transcribed while in a state of trance.

If séance participants wanted physical manifestations of spirit contact, there was also something called "slate writing." The technique consisted of the medium and the attendee seated opposite each other at a small table. Each would hold a side or a corner of a blank slate in a wooden frame like those typically used by schoolchildren. The slate was then pressed against the underside of the table. Between the slate and the table, a piece of chalk was placed for use by the spirit writer. If a scratching noise was heard a short time later, it meant that the spirit was writing something on the slate. When the process was completed, raps were heard, the slate was turned over, and there would be a message – supposedly written by the spirits.

Although slate writing was often criticized as fraudulent, it remained popular throughout the nineteenth century. There is no question that it was susceptible to trickery, which was proven by scores of magicians in the early 1900s. Even so, there were an estimated 2,000 "writing mediums" all over America who claimed they wrote down, under spirit control, messages communicated to them from the other side.

The planchette was another form of spirit communication that was popularized in France in the mid-1850s and soon became a lasting favorite on both sides of the Atlantic. French for "little planks," the first planchettes were heart-shaped devices made from wood with three small wheels on the bottom. The point of the heart held a small, downward-facing pencil. The idea was for the medium to place his or her hand on the planchette and then the pencil would write out messages from the spirit that was controlling the medium. When the planchette became available in American in 1868, it was an immediate sensation and thousands were sold. It was the forerunner of the immensely popular Ouija board. To what extent the messages obtained are from spirits or from unconscious activity by the person holding the planchette is still debated today.

Direct voice phenomena, like automatic writing, was supposedly produced by the spirits without the intervention of the medium. One favorite test of the debunkers was to have a medium fill her mouth with water while the discarnate entity spoke. Assuming that the medium had no assistant hiding nearby to create a second voice, this was one way of determining whether or not any trickery was involved. In some cases, two distinct voices were heard, one presumed to come from the medium and one from the spirit. Several mediums confounded skeptics with "direct voice" phenomena, particularly in the days before recordings.

As time passed, those with a need to contact the spirit world continued to search for other ways with which to do it. Around the time when recording devices came into practical use, psychical researchers began searching for ways to capture the voices of the dead. The first experimenters were using gramophones and wax cylinders, but the first recording of a spirit voice on actual tape was achieved by Reverend Drayton Thomas who, during his investigations of the spirit medium Gladys Osborne Leonard in the 1940s, captured an audible, disembodied voice during a séance. He later came to believe that the voice was that of his dead father.

The practice of attempting to record spirit voices grew in popularity, beginning in the 1950s, with the increased availability of portable tape recorders The voices came to be known as Electronic Voice Phenomena (EVP). These sounds are apparently sonic events of unknown origin, which can be heard, and sometimes captured in recordings, on various types of electronic apparatus, including tape recorders and even radio equipment. The voices on the tapes take on diverse forms, sometimes seeming to speak in tongues, singing or speaking in gibberish. The messages often make a sort of backward sense, as though communication is difficult. They can also apparently speak directly to researchers and call them by name. They can be heard over telephones and as anomalous interference on tape recordings. Some of them seen to enjoy engaging in dialogue, answering questions or supplying personal information about the researchers, possibly as a way of establishing credibility.

The psychic Attila von Szalay, a professional photographer who often claimed to hear disembodied voices in the air around him, started researching EVP with paranormal researcher Raymond Bayless in the early 1950s. Their initial attempts with a 78-rpm record cutter and player were disappointing. Regardless, they continued their efforts using a device that Bayless invented. It consisted of a box with an interior microphone resting inside an old-fashioned speaking trumpet. The microphone cord led out of the box and connected to a tape recorder. Almost immediately, the researchers began to hear whispers originating from inside the box, which they managed to record. Von Szalay carried on taping for many years using an open microphone connected to a reel-to-reel recorder.

Around 1959, Friederich Jurgenson, a retired Swedish opera singer, film producer and bird watcher, was recording bird songs in the woods near his home. When he played back his tapes, he discovered that strange, garbled fragments of human speech had somehow made their way onto the recording. This was in spite of the fact that he was sure that he had been completely alone when the recording was made. He allegedly recognized one of the voices as that of his dead mother, saying in German: "Friedrich, you are being watched. Friedel, my little Friedel, can you hear me?" As he listened to the tapes, he found that the voices spoke in different languages. Also, he noted that longer phrases spoken by the mysterious voices often had improper structure and bad grammar and in some cases, the syllables were stretched or compressed in a way that made it hard to understand what was being said. The strangest aspect of all was the eerie way that the voices seemed to reply to comments that Jurgenson inadvertently made. He began to hold conversations with the voices by recording questions and then later searching the tapes for answers. In 1963, after four years of recording, he gave a press conference about his findings and published a book about the strange communications. His conclusion was that the tape recorder acted as a form of electronic link to the realm of the dead.

There was resurgence in interest in EVP in the 1970s and 1980s, led by a researcher named Sarah Estep, who spent more than fifteen years recording and classifying various types of voices. She developed a system for the recorded voices, breaking them down in levels from easily understandable messages to barely discernible noises.

But, as it was in the early days when simple knocks were no longer enough to satisfy the curiosity of those hoping to establish a link with the other side, basic recording devices have been nearly abandoned as researchers seek other methods of contacting the spirit world. Instrumental Transcommunication (ITC) is defined as using technical means to receive meaningful spirit messages. The ITC method originated as a form of EVP but encompasses a myriad of techniques to try and make contact with the spirit world using television, radios, telephones, computers and the popular "ghost boxes" – whose origins began in the 1950s.

At that time, some researchers began developing theories concerning radio waves as a way to contact the dead. Short-lived inventions like the "Spiricom" and "Psychfon" began trying to use radio technology, but with mixed results. In the early 2000s, new devices were created that used a white noise generator, an amplifier, a small sound chamber, a microphone and a radio receiver to purportedly communicate with the dead. The device was designed to tune through radio stations along the dial, catching them for a few seconds. The words that are heard as the device slowly tunes along the dial are combined with the sound of static to provide a method for spirits to communicate with the living.

And, as you'll read later in this book, these "boxes" will not be the final method used to communicate with the other side. Like Spiritualism and psychical research, the ways in which we contact the next world will continue to change, mutate and adapt, along with the technology that we have at our disposal.

April Slaughter has been speaking to the dead for most of her life. She has worked tirelessly to investigate the many methods and claims that have come along over the years and finally, she's presenting it all in this book. I can promise you that – no matter what you might personally believe – you've never read a book quite like this one before. Sure, there have been plenty of other books about spirit communication that have been released over the years, but none of them are like this one. It's unique, it's well researched and it's one that will leave you thinking. Trust me... no matter what you *think* you already know about spirits and the next world, you'll be startled by this book.

So, read on. All that I ask is that you keep an open mind and even if what you read unnerves you, you'll remember it long after you close the final pages of this book.

Troy Taylor
Spring 2013

INTRODUCTION

Everybody loves a good ghost story. There is something inside each of us that gravitates toward the mystery of the unknown. We flock to scary movies knowing (and hoping) that we'll see something that will make us jump out of our seats. We buy books by authors who possess the talent of getting under our skin with their fictional tales of angry spirits seeking revenge on the living. Fear is big business. Unfortunately, it is also the one thing I battle with the most in the work that I do; and trust me, it *is* work.

A large majority of people would consider me a "ghost hunter," and while this is true in part, there is much more to the goings-on than initially meets the eye. I don't actually hunt ghosts. I don't have their heads mounted on the wall above my fireplace. The label is misleading, but it is how the public at large has come to identify those of us who spend our nights wandering through old abandoned buildings and skulking around cemeteries. I will admit that for many years, that is exactly what I did. I have long been fascinated by ghosts, by the idea that I could be all alone somewhere, and yet surrounded by things I couldn't see.

People who have worked with me will tell you that I am largely unafraid of walking into dark places, of encountering someone or something that may or may not be receptive to the intrusion. I assure you, however, that this was not always the case. If ever there had been born a child who was truly terrified of her own shadow, that child was me. When I was younger, everything frightened me. I never took risks, even if those risks meant that I might have a little fun. I didn't want to learn how to swim for fear I'd drown. When I turned sixteen, and all of my peers were begging for a car of their own, I was dreading getting behind the wheel. So, if the boogeyman truly existed, I knew beyond a shadow of a doubt that he would find his way to me eventually. Obviously, I've since outgrown many of my fears, but not before being absolutely consumed by them.

The idea to write this book manifested years ago, but it has evolved from how I first envisioned it. Initially, it was simply to be a guide on the various ways of making contact with the dead, using different tools and techniques. I had not planned to include details of my own personal experiences, at least not to any great extent. There was a time I did not believe they were relatable, or perhaps even relevant to anyone other than myself. I used to believe that avoiding the personal side of things was the more "professional" route to take, but with every new experience I have, the more responsibility I feel to share it.

Several years ago, I was asked to give a presentation at a local library. I had only expected a dozen or so people to attend, and was stunned to find that nearly every seat in the fairly large conference room was filled. About halfway through the presentation, a woman seated near the back of the room raised her hand with a question.

"What exactly do you hope to gain by doing this sort of thing? Do you honestly think you're going to convince anyone that you're actually talking to ghosts?" she asked, in a more than slightly irritated tone.

While I had been fairly used to skepticism by that point in my career, I had never had anyone openly question my personal motivations, especially not in front of so many other people. I remember this moment so vividly because it forced me to look inward and to formulate an answer that was complete, articulate, and above all else, honest.

"I have no desire to convince anyone of anything," I answered. "I know what I have experienced, and how it has impacted my life. I share my story hoping it will inspire other people to push beyond their fears and find out for themselves what the truth really is."

The expression on the woman's face softened, as I think she had expected a very different - and perhaps defensive - answer. She did not press further, and I picked up right where I had left off with my speech. As the presentation came to a close, several people approached to introduce themselves and to exchange a quick thought or two on the material.

As the number of people in line dwindled, the woman who had asked whether I expected to convince people of the existence of ghosts extended her hand and thanked me for answering her question. She apologized for interrupting, and explained that she had become extremely frustrated in recent years by people who claimed they had irrefutable evidence that ghosts exist. Nothing she had seen or heard had been able to convince her that spirits were among us, or that they could interact with the living. She was pleasantly surprised that I did not claim to possess such proof.

The data that I have collected and shared over the years is impressive... *to me.* While I am convinced of its authenticity, I certainly do not expect anyone else to take my word for it. It is fairly obvious that many people are just looking for an argument. They want to be challenged, and to be engaged in a war of words. Such individuals are often initially disappointed with my reaction to their disbelief in the supernatural, as I encourage them to continue on in doubt if that is what makes them the most comfortable.

This is how I have always approached my research, and I encourage anyone with a curiosity to learn to go and do just that. Ask questions, challenge ideas, find out for yourself what really exists out there in the "unknown." If you happen to reach a different conclusion than I did, so be it. I hold more respect for people who've dug for paranormal treasure and never found it than for those who've never even bothered to pick up the shovel.

There is a great deal of misinformation out there, at least in my view, and it has become a constant source of frustration. Let's face it – there is a stigma attached to what I do, to what many people in the paranormal field do. I have been called a witch, a necromancer, and other names not suitable to mention; all this, before being given the chance to explain myself, my methods, and my motivations.

I believe people react the way they do because they are afraid. Fear holds them back from learning more about what really happens when a person on this side of the veil establishes a connection with one (or more) on the other side. Ask most anyone what they think of Ouija boards, for example, and nine out of ten times you're going to get the all-too-common "they're instruments of evil" response. Even if they've never attempted to use one, have no knowledge of where or how they originated, the frightening stories people have heard about them keep them from accepting any other view.

The fear is understandable; it was a weight I personally lived under for the first part of my life. Eventually, I came to the realization that if I was going to fear something, I should probably learn everything I could about it to better protect myself from any perceived danger. In chasing after and studying the very things that scared me the most, I learned not only to survive them, but that there really wasn't anything to fear in the first place. I could have remained ignorant, but I would have denied myself years of uplifting and life-affirming experiences. Yes, the dead have taught me to appreciate life. They've proven to me that I am never truly alone in this world, and that while death will eventually find me, it isn't going to erase me.

It has to be mentioned that my journey through all of this has not been without its difficulties and disappointments. Some of the most heart-wrenching incidents in my life have occurred while delving into paranormal research, and I have learned some heavy lessons as a result. There have been numerous occasions that have nearly convinced me to throw in the towel, to close the door and walk away from all of it; life would certainly be less stressful if I chose that course. However, I've found that I'm always drawn back in because I truly believe I am doing the work I was destined to do. Whether you are a skeptic, a believer, or someone who finds themselves floating comfortably somewhere in between, it is my sincere hope that the overall message of this book will reach you in one way or another. Every individual with curiosity about the other side is uniquely motivated to pursue their own answers.

I'm not going to claim that every bump in the night has a supernatural origin. In fact, I believe the majority of them do not. However, when a legitimate phenomenon occurs, I think we should remind ourselves to be open to the possibility that something positive can be gained from the event. Perhaps the details of my experiences will inspire people within the paranormal community (and without) to realize that there are greater implications to being "connected" than capturing the next great ghost photo or disembodied voice. There is a bigger picture to view; it's just a matter of opening your eyes and being willing to see it.

April Slaughter
Spring 2013

–I–
The People in the Basement

"The oldest and strongest emotion of mankind is fear,
and the oldest and strongest kind of fear is fear of the unknown."
H.P. Lovecraft

I grew up in a haunted house. While this is not the most unique beginning to a story, it is nonetheless the truthful beginning to mine. Many people who become active in the paranormal community have experienced things in their lives that they couldn't explain, things that left them frightened or that challenged their belief in the existence of an afterlife, and I am no exception.

I was born and raised in northern Utah, the youngest of four children. The first several years of my life were largely (and thankfully) uneventful, but things changed when I turned eight years old, and my father's job required the family to relocate. We didn't have to move far, but at that age, even moving just a little over an hour away seemed like a great distance to me.

As my parents began their search for the perfect new home in the perfect new neighborhood, they came across one in particular that my mother fell instantly in love with. It was by no means a large or elaborate home, but it was – and continues to be – beautiful. An elderly couple had been the only people to occupy the house, and they were no longer able to keep up with the demands of owning and maintaining it due to age and various medical issues.

During my mother's initial tour through the two-level house, she noticed how meticulously well-kept it was.

"You have a beautiful home," she said to the elderly woman. "Everything is so organized and tidy."

Her response caught my mother a little off guard.

"I keep it that way because angels pass through here," she replied.

While it struck my mother as a little bizarre, she didn't think much of the comment and continued on with her tour. My parents made an offer on the house, and before I knew it, we were moving in. There was nothing about the house that would have set off alarm bells for anyone else, but it felt *different* to me. At the time, I thought my resistance to the move was simply born out of my anxiety about starting over somewhere new. As it turned out, the house *was* different, and I was the only one picking up on it.

My father and grandfather had worked on a large room in the basement, constructing a wall to divide it into two separate bedrooms. My brother claimed the smaller of the two, and I shared the larger one with one of my sisters. It had two doorways leading into it, but they were not framed to hang doors. This left our room open to the hallway, at the other end of which was a bathroom and a basement living room.

I remember lying in my twin bed that first night in the house, staring into the darkened hallway, imagining that all manner of horrible monsters were lurking out there waiting for me to fall asleep before swooping in to steal me away. Having my sister in the room with me was no comfort, as she and I never really got along that well. If it came down to her or me, I was sure she wouldn't hesitate to throw me to the monsters.

I woke up the next morning with all of my fingers and all of my toes, not a single drop of blood spilt, and with every hair in its proper place. I had seen and heard nothing out of the ordinary. Still, every night approached with the same sense of dread, and every morning I woke up thinking I might be able to overcome it in time.

Illuminating the Shadows

As a child, I had a vivid imagination that could rival anyone's. Easily frightened by the simplest of things, I was a steady and reliable source of entertainment for my older siblings. They knew that if they wanted to get a rise out of me, they most certainly would.

My brother (the oldest of the four) would often convince me to sit and watch scary movies with him, only to torture me with the storyline afterward. Every monster I had seen on the screen was real, and was hiding in my closet or underneath my bed. I suppose any "normal" child would have grown suspicious after awhile, but I trusted my brother implicitly and he knew it. Freddy Krueger, Gremlins, Ghoulies, even Killer Tomatoes – you name it; they were all out to get me.

Thus was born my absolute terror of the dark. An obvious solution (and one that may have alleviated the problem altogether for other kids) would be to use a night-light. Certainly, no monster wanted to be seen. They were allergic to light, right? At least Gremlins were, anyway. They turned into puddles of goo whenever the slightest amount of light touched them. I had hoped this unwritten rule would somehow apply to the myriad of other monsters that were just waiting to jump out at me.

So, I plugged in a night-light and placed all of my faith in it to protect me. I must have thought that all of the strange noises I heard at night would somehow suddenly stop occurring as well. It is odd to think that a little light made me feel that safe. My false sense of security would turn out to be short-lived. After all, light helps you to see... and I wasn't prepared to *see* anything.

One evening, after having only been asleep for an hour or two, I heard a whispery voice speak my name from out in the hallway, just beyond my bedroom.

"April..."

I must have been sleeping fairly deeply, as it took me quite a while to pull myself out of the grogginess and focus. My night-light illuminated the hallway just enough for me to see that someone was standing there, looking at me. I was awake *now*.

This person in the hallway was not a member of my family. The figure stood about five and a half feet tall, but had no distinguishable features; at least, none that I remembered in the one or two seconds I gave myself to actually look at it. I instantly threw the covers up over my head and began to pray that whoever (or whatever) was in the hallway would vanish. I cannot recall how long I kept my head buried in the blankets, but I do know it felt like an eternity. When I finally mustered up enough courage to peek out, the figure was gone.

Had I been dreaming? I certainly thought I had been when I awoke the next morning and everything was fine. If a ghost – or something else – had really been there, would it have left me alone simply because I had buried my face in the covers? I doubted it. It had to have been a dream. It would not happen again.

Right.

For several nights after that, a sort of panic took over me as bedtime approached. We hadn't lived in the house for all that long, so I was still fairly uncomfortable sleeping in the basement, even if I did have my all-powerful night-light.

It could have been a matter of days, or weeks – I don't know for sure – but the figure once again appeared in the hallway. This time, it stood at the bottom of the staircase that led into the basement and directly into my room. The terror that ripped through me had me so paralyzed that I couldn't react and pull the covers up over my head like I had before. I couldn't move. I couldn't scream. I just laid there and stared at it, completely unable to look away. After a few moments, it stepped out of sight, only to show up at the other entrance at the far side of my bedroom.

Then, it just disappeared. It didn't walk away. It didn't fade away. It just wasn't there anymore.

After my second encounter with the entity, I not only lost faith in the power of my night-light to protect me, but I woke up the next morning and immediately threw it into the trash. The dark was not my enemy; it was my friend. The night-light had only taken a nightmarish thing from my imagination and made it real and visible. The dark would allow me to dismiss a bump in the night as something with a plausible explanation.

And so once again my world went dark, and I hoped that would be the end of it. It wasn't.

Just Beyond the Bathroom Door

The events that took place in the basement of my childhood home became "normal" to me. This isn't to say that I enjoyed them; I certainly didn't. They were just something that I learned to accept. My family was thoroughly entertained (and just as thoroughly unconvinced) by my tales of apparitions and strange noises, but it wouldn't always stay that way. I think in the back of everyone's minds, they knew it was possible that our house was haunted; they just didn't want to *know* that it was. I can't say that I blame them. I was having a difficult time with that fact myself.

One early Saturday morning when I was about ten or eleven, my mother was busy getting ready to host a yard sale. Everyone was told to gather what items they no longer wanted or needed and to bring them outside. I have never been (and will probably never be) what you would call a morning person. My siblings were running all over the house, and all I wanted to do was catch a little more shut-eye. I begrudgingly rolled out of bed and walked into the bathroom, not more than just a few steps from my bedroom. I pushed the door behind me, intending to close it all the way, but it didn't quite latch. I didn't care, as I was just going to brush my teeth before heading back to my room to change.

As I was looking in the mirror, a quick flash of light appeared behind me. I spun around to look in the direction from which it came and saw nothing. As I turned back to the mirror, I looked out into the hallway from the gap in the doorway and saw two people walking past. One was a man, probably around thirty years of age, holding a little boy's hand. The boy couldn't have been older than five or six. Both individuals had dark hair, light skin, and wore identical navy blue striped polo shirts. They were headed in the direction of the basement living room, which I referred to as the "dead animal room," where my father displayed many of his hunting trophies. My first thought was that my mother must have sent these people into the basement to look at an item they might be interested in purchasing. I immediately pulled the bathroom door open and walked out just as the man and the boy passed, and saw no one. Where could they have gone? They could not have walked into the living room and back out again without my having seen them. They were just gone. I was puzzled, but returned to my room to get dressed and then walked upstairs to inquire about the strangers who had been in the house.

I found my parents shuffling through things for the yard sale out on the front lawn. I asked, "Who were the two people in the identical striped shirts I saw in the basement?"

They both looked perplexed. They had not let anyone into the house. I was teased for months afterward about the incident. Anytime I went looking around for something, my father would say, "Maybe the guys in the matching striped shirts took it." I realized fairly quickly that it was probably best to keep my strange experiences to myself if no one was going to take them seriously.

A week or so passed, and things were quiet in the house. I hadn't seen or heard anything unusual, and I began to hope that perhaps all the nonsense was over with. Maybe whoever or whatever had taken up residence in the basement decided it was time to move on. Another morning came, and my sluggish routine began again. This time as I went into the bathroom, I made sure to close and lock the door behind me. After brushing my teeth, I got into the shower, hoping the hot water would lift me out of my sleepy morning fog.

BAM!! BAM!! BAM!!

Three loud bangs on the bathroom door startled me so much that I nearly fell down in the shower. With the water still running, I jumped out, grabbed a towel and yelled, "What? Who's out there?" No one answered. I looked at the doorknob and saw it was moving back and forth, as though someone on the other side were trying to see if it was locked. I asked again, "Who's out there?" Nothing. Once my heart rate slowed a bit, I closed the shower door thinking that one of my sisters probably wanted to get something in the bathroom and had walked away after realizing I had locked the door.

BAM!! BAM!! BAM!!

Again? The banging was even louder this time. I quickly went from being startled to being angry. "GO AWAY!" I shouted. The doorknob shook again, but I ignored it. Whoever was on the other side of that door was just going to have to wait their turn. I finished washing up and got dressed, without thinking too much of the incident until I began asking everyone in the house who it was who had been so rudely insistent on getting into the bathroom. No one admitted to even being in the basement, let alone banging on the door. Somebody was lying, I was sure of it. I tried not to let it bother me, until it happened again the very next day... and the next... and the next, always when I was in the shower.

I thought I must have been going crazy. Why were these things happening in the house, and why were they happening just around me? Why was it limited to the basement? By then, fear had become my constant companion. I had no idea what to do about it, or if there were anything *to* do about it. I spoke to my mother about the repeated banging on the bathroom door, but she seemed unconcerned, so I just learned to drop it. Talking about it wasn't going to solve anything.

The bathroom in the basement also served as the laundry room, so my mother was often putting a load of clothing in the washer, and pulling another out of the dryer. Several weeks after my first experience with the banging on the bathroom door, my mother went downstairs to tend to the laundry while I sat upstairs at the dining room table doing my homework. Ten or fifteen minutes passed, and my mother came back up the stairs looking more than a little confused.

"Did you need something?" she asked me.

"No, why?" I replied.

"Someone was just banging on the bathroom door," she said.

I didn't know what to say, so I just stared blankly at her and shook my head. I wanted to say, *See? I told you something strange was going on*, but I held my tongue and went back to focusing on my homework. Days later, my mother would report that it happened to her again while no one else was home. She began to wonder if what I had been telling her was true. There *were* people in the basement. The question was what could be done about it?

Silence Was Not the Solution

The more I told people what was happening in the house, the more they distanced themselves from me. Friends, family members, anyone… they didn't want to hear about it. It is always easier to pretend things do not exist if you don't experience them yourself. I stopped talking about it. I felt entirely isolated.

Ghosts, spirits, angels, whatever you want to call them – they were in my house. They were in the basement with me. My silence made everyone else feel more at ease, but it only made me feel desperately lost. My fear had subsided some, simply out of getting used to the frequency of events, but I was still keenly aware that I was part of something I had absolutely no control over. I simply accepted the facts as I knew them, and did my best to just keep on living in spite of them.

Years passed, and I eventually became the only child with a bedroom in the basement. Odd things kept happening. Objects would move themselves in my room. Doors would inexplicably open and close. Lights would turn on and off without anyone flipping a switch.

I grew tired of watching shadows wandering in the hallway just outside of my room as I'd lie in bed at night. I approached my father and asked if he would frame the two entryways to the room and hang doors for me, under the guise that I needed a bit more privacy. Being alone in the basement, this wasn't really an issue, but he didn't argue with me about it. Within days I had doors.

I made a trip to the hardware store and bought two door handles with locks, each requiring its own key. Dad installed them for me, though he wasn't too thrilled with the idea that I would be locking him out of a section of his own house. He must have wondered what I intended to keep hidden in there, but since I was a good kid (and by good, I mean ridiculously well-behaved) he didn't make too much of a fuss. He trusted me and I appreciated it.

I knew the doors were not going to keep anything out (or in), but they provided me with a certain sense of security. I was doing the only thing I thought could be done for any measure of relief, no matter how small. I locked the doors every night before I crawled into bed, and tucked the keys under my pillow. Many mornings, I'd wake to find the bedroom doors open. The keys had never been misplaced, nor had there been an opportunity for anyone to have duplicates made. Nevertheless, the locked doors were opening without keys, and I didn't understand how that could be possible.

I was running out of ideas. The only thing I could think to do was to verbally ask "them" to stop opening my doors at night. I begged, sometimes at the point of tears, for it to end. I didn't actually expect it to work, but it did, temporarily, anyway.

My doors didn't open on their own anymore, but another phenomenon quickly arose in its place. I began waking up in the mornings covered in bruises. They never appeared on my head or face, but the rest of my body would often be marked with them. I had never awakened during the night feeling anything or anyone touching me, nor did I feel any soreness from the bruises upon their discovery. There had been no rhyme or reason to it. They were just *there*. I tried not to think about them. I even tried to keep them hidden, but eventually they caught my mother's attention. She questioned me repeatedly about how I had gotten them. Was I falling? Had someone at school been physically aggressive with me? I didn't have an explanation for her, so she went looking for one on her own.

Mom had worked in the medical field as a phlebotomist for years, so her first inclination was to have blood samples submitted for testing. She had a suspicion that I might be suffering from a bleeding disorder called von Willebrand disease. Every test that could be done was done, and none of them ever came back with anything other than normal results. I was by all accounts a healthy young girl, but the bruises just kept coming. I didn't know if the "people in the basement" were causing them, but I couldn't say for certain that they weren't somehow responsible. I did not believe anything in the house had actually intended to harm me. I had never seen, heard, or felt anything that would explain the appearance of the bruises.

My mother continued to worry about me, so instead of choking back my suspicions, I decided it would be best to tell her that I thought something in the basement was trying to get my attention. I confided in her about the doors opening by themselves at night, and how I had asked the spirits to stop doing it. The only thing I could think of was to once again ask them to stop. I did, and the bruises never came back.

Suddenly, I realized that keeping silent was no longer the best plan. At least my mother was listening to me now. The bruising went away, but as I had learned from past experience, asking the spirits to cease one activity usually resulted in another one taking its place.

The Boogeyman

Nothing terrified me more growing up than the idea of being left at home alone, especially at night. Both of my parents worked and my older siblings had little to no time or interest in looking after me. Everyone had their own lives to lead, and trying to reassure an overly anxious kid didn't rank all that high on anyone's list of priorities. I can't say that I blame them.

I was beginning to get used to the people in the basement. You could even say that I often enjoyed having them around. If I was home by myself, I knew I really wasn't alone. The strange incidents that had once plagued me became an unexpected source of comfort. My anxieties about being left at home alone had nothing to do with the disembodied voices or the random opening and closing of doors. I didn't care that the lights turned on by themselves, or that the stereo system would begin blaring out of nowhere. This was what I knew, what I had grown up with. This was my normal.

With each passing year, my attitude began to shift from fearing the dead to fearing the living. After all, those with a pulse and a desire to hurt you have a higher probability of doing so than those who have passed on.

Being home alone always scared me, but it became especially stressful when I was left alone at night. We lived adjacent to a busy highway leading into a canyon just behind the house. I was always worried that a stranger would try to break in.

Whenever the weather was halfway decent, every window in the house would be left open to catch the breeze coming down from the mountains. All of the doors had locks, but none of them were especially difficult to manipulate. At times when I had found myself locked out, all I had to do was remove a screen, push against the glass, and any window became an entrance.

One evening, my fears about being home alone would prove themselves justified. My parents had gone out to dinner with friends, and my brother and sisters were nowhere to be found. I had nowhere to go, so I was going to have to get through the night on my own. I was old enough to look after myself, of course, but I preferred having someone else around.

My father had claimed my brother's old bedroom in the basement and had converted it into an office. On this particular evening, I thought I would pass the time by playing games on the computer until somebody came home. Just as my nerves were beginning to calm a bit, something caught my attention. My eyes instantly locked on the door that led into the yard on the far side of the house. The doorknob was slowly turning. The door was locked as always, but I knew there was someone on the other side testing to see whether or not it would budge.

I froze. I couldn't move. I couldn't tear my eyes away from the doorknob. Panic shot through me worse than any I had ever felt before. In that instant, I knew that if someone outside wanted to gain entry, they would most certainly be able to. All of the windows upstairs were open, as it had been unbearably hot and we did not have central air conditioning. I didn't know if I had locked the front door. I wasn't near a phone. I would have to run upstairs if I had any hope of calling the police.

The doorknob stopped moving and my fear was all the more amplified. Whoever was out there was sure to try and find another way in. I had to move. I had to run. In an instant, I bolted out of the office and ran faster than I ever had in my life. As I reached the top of the stairs, I saw something that threw me into a state of confusion. Every window in the house was closed, every curtain drawn. How did that happen? I was the only one there, and I certainly hadn't done it.

I ran to the front door. It was locked. A few seconds passed, and the doorknob shook just like the one in the basement had. I was right; the would-be intruder was moving around the exterior of the house trying to find a way in. I ran to the kitchen counter and grabbed the phone to dial 911 in a breathless panic. As I stood there, begging the dispatcher to send someone out to the house, several lights on the upstairs level of the house simultaneously turned on.

Within minutes, a squad car came speeding into the driveway. I stayed on the line with the dispatcher as two officers made their way around the house looking for anything suspicious. They found nothing. I reported to them that I had seen the doorknobs shaking, but I made no mention of the windows locking themselves or the lights inexplicably turning on. How would I have explained that?

The officers assured me that they would keep close to the house for the remainder of the evening and wished me a good night. As I closed the door, a wave of exhaustion poured over me. I took a couple of steps and sat down on the kitchen floor. Never before had I been that frightened. I took a few deep breaths, and tried to wrap my head around the evening's events. How had every point of entry in the house been secured without my having done it? I could only think of one explanation: the people in the basement.

In that moment, I knew I had nothing to fear from whatever was with me in the house. Whoever they were, however many of them there were, they had transformed from foe to friend. The boogeyman was not a phantom of my imagination, rather a living, breathing person who would have most likely done more harm to me than any specter I had encountered in the house. Little by little, appreciation replaced fear.

As the years passed, I learned that I could never predict when paranormal phenomena would occur in the house. It would often happen for days on end and then stop altogether for months at a time. There was no rhyme or reason to any of it. All I knew for certain was that I wasn't in any danger. Granted, it took years to come to that realization, but being at peace with it made living with *them* a great deal easier. It was an eventful, yet peaceful co-existence.

A Growing Curiosity

As my fears subsided, my desire to learn more about the phenomena I was experiencing grew. I sought out and devoured books by the dozens, hoping the information contained within would help me to further expand my understanding of spirit interaction. There were novels and other ghost-themed works of fiction, but they did not provide me with any real answers. I needed to delve into the history of spirit communication in order to understand how to divide fact from fiction. I thought it would be simple, but as is often the case in the realm of the unknown, that dividing line would be difficult to identify.

Spiritualists in the early and mid-nineteenth century were known for putting on quite a show for those interested in making contact with the deceased. They found opportunities to not only provide that experience for others, but to profit from it as well; and profit they did. Fraud was prevalent, and while many worked to expose it, there were still large numbers of desperate people who wanted to believe they were talking and interacting with their lost loved ones. Whether or not they actually were was another question entirely. Those who stood to gain financially from defrauding the public did so with little to no regard for the bereaved. As long as the money was rolling in, the show would go on. Fraudulent practices aside, at least a fraction of the accounts had to have some truth to them, didn't they?

Having seen apparitions and heard their voices in my childhood home, I knew that the existence of ghosts or spirits was a reality. While I no longer feared their presence, I wasn't willing to try and conduct a séance of my own to speak to them. I'd never have the courage to ask my parents to allow a Ouija board into the house, let alone ask anyone else to participate in such an attempt. I had no desire to try automatic writing, and I certainly didn't know of any psychics to talk to. To me, the possibility of opening up a two-way communication channel with the spirits in the house began to seem less and less likely.

Things would have to remain as they were, despite my frustration. Without the support of those around me, I felt as though I didn't have any other option than to simply accept the situation, continue to live with it as best I could, and move on with my life.

-2-
Hello? Is Anybody There?

"If I can talk to a seeming entity, and if it can answer me, I am justified in considering it a reality."
X, Letters From the Afterlife

When I was twenty years old, I met and married a Navy man who was stationed on North Island in San Diego, California. I didn't think much of the move I'd be required to make, except that I was excited to begin a new chapter of my life and spend time in a place I'd only briefly visited before.

I can't say I had any real concern for my family back home, or how the paranormal activity in the house might or might not affect them. There was a part of me, however, that was sad to leave the spirits in the house. Having been an introvert most of my life up until that point, they had become familiar to me, even comforting. I wondered what would occupy their time, or if they would even notice that I was no longer around.

Several months after the move, my mother called to tell me that something strange had happened to her in the basement. She was sure she had heard (and felt) someone unseen breathing into her ear. She was a little shaken by it, and wanted to know if I had any idea why something like that would have happened. There wasn't much I could say other than I didn't think there was anything in the house that meant to do her or anyone else harm. From time to time she would call to report some other strange occurrence, and I'd do my best to comfort her. We didn't talk about ghosts and such very often, but I was grateful to my mother for being open enough to broach the subject with me when she was worried.

Nothing terribly extraordinary happened in the house until my maternal grandmother Jeri came to stay with my parents for a short visit. My mother had converted my old bedroom into a guest room, and Grandma settled in and made herself at home.

Early one morning during my grandmother's visit, my mother called to tell me she had a story even I might have a hard time believing. Everyone in the house had been asleep the night before, when my grandmother came upstairs to wake my mother in the middle of the night.

"She was wide awake and completely coherent," she said. "Grandma told me there were people walking through the bedroom, repeatedly waking her up. She wanted me to come downstairs and ask these people to leave her alone so that she could get some rest."

My grandmother had never been privy to my experiences in the house. My family didn't talk much about it with me, let alone anyone else. When she woke my mother for assistance, she was under the impression that living, breathing individuals were randomly walking through the bedroom at all hours of the night. It had her confused, frustrated, and more than just a little unnerved.

"I asked her who she had seen in the basement," said my mother. "Through the course of the night she said she'd seen two women, a man, and even a dog. Several times she had addressed these people directly, but she grew quite irritated when they didn't respond to her. She didn't appreciate being ignored and she thought I would have better luck at getting them to leave her alone."

My mother never encountered the women, the man, or the dog that my grandmother had seen, but she was well aware that such things had occurred in the house in the past. She reassured my grandmother that all would be well, and no further incident occurred during her visit.

It was after this particular event that I really began to feel a growing desire to know more about what was happening back home. I knew nobody had anything really to fear in the house, but I was no longer satisfied with simply knowing the house was haunted. I wanted to know *why* it was. I had read countless books on the subject of ghosts and the existence of life after death, and I had certainly experienced my fair share of what I believed to be legitimate supernatural phenomena, but I desired a deeper understanding of the rhyme and reason of it all.

The spirits at home, while they had kept me company for a number of years, were not the spirits of people I had known and loved. They were largely strangers to me, albeit benevolent ones, and I had not yet begun to imagine what it would be like to reach out and connect with a loved one after their passing. That day would come, however, and much sooner than I realized.

Visits from Grandma

On December 23, 2000 my husband and I were in Utah visiting family for the Christmas holiday. He and I had traveled to Ogden to visit with and deliver gifts to my paternal grandparents, Reed and Marilyn. It had been snowing for days, so we felt it best to brave the weather instead of asking them to travel in it.

Grandpa was sitting in his usual spot on the couch watching television while Grandma and I caught up on all of the things that had happened to me since relocating from Utah to California the year before. As we sat talking, I noticed something strange. For most of

My Grandmother Marilyn

my life, my grandmother had opted to wear a wig. She had the most beautiful silken white hair, which I hardly ever had the opportunity to see as she kept it hidden away. She complained that it was too fine and difficult to work with at her age. I often lamented to her about how gorgeous her hair was and how I had missed seeing it, but it only landed on deaf ears, and the wig seemed a permanent fixture. On this particular evening, and without explanation, she had chosen not to wear it. I didn't make anything of it at the time, as I was just happy to see her as the natural beauty that she was.

As the evening wore on, Grandma asked me to follow her down the hall into her room to look at several afghans she had made. She had always crocheted the most beautifully intricate blankets, and I had coveted them all of my life.

"Pick which one you would like to take home with you," she said. "Everyone else will have to wait to pick theirs, but you can choose yours now."

My heart sank. She had always told the grandchildren that the blankets would be given to each of us after she passed, and not a moment before. I hesitated. I did not want to think about it. My grandmother had been there all of my life, and I was content with the illusion that she would always be there. She insisted I choose an afghan, so I reached for the one I had always loved the most. I tried to convince myself that she was just feeling generous, and that it meant nothing ominous.

She then sat me down on the edge of her bed and showed me her wedding ring. I knew the story of how my grandfather had proposed, but she told me again. Grandpa had asked her to marry him several times, and she had always turned him down. She had been married once before and was not at all interested in going down that road again. After his continued persistence, she told him she would accept his proposal on one condition – he would have to buy her a flawless one-carat diamond. She was fully aware that my grandfather did not have the means to facilitate such a request, and thus the never-ending proposals would most likely end. She was wrong. It took every last resource he had, but he bought her that diamond, and she made good on her promise to accept. They were married for nearly 60 years, and loved each other deeply each and every one of them.

After repeating this story, she said, "Now, I am not to be buried with this diamond. Make sure I am buried with my wedding band, but not the diamond. It is to be kept in the family."

I didn't know what to say to her. Why was she telling me this? She was only 79. Surely she would be around for several more years. I tried hard not to cry, but a tear or two slipped out anyway. She walked me through the house, pointing out different things and instructing me as to whom they were to go.

After several hours, it was time for me leave. It was always Grandma's routine to walk me to the front door and watch from the step as I got into my car. This night, however, she braved the ice-slicked driveway and walked me all the way to my car. She cradled my face in her hands, looked me in the eye, and said, "I love you very much, April."

As I drove away, I thought about all of the little things that were different about this visit. I tried to ignore the nagging feeling that I would never see her again, but as it would turn out, it was indeed the last time I saw her alive.

My mother made a trip out to California the following February to spend a few days with me sight-seeing and enjoying each other's company. We had just purchased tickets to see an afternoon matinee when my father called with devastating news. My grandmother had suddenly passed away at home. We immediately made arrangements for my mother to return to

Utah, and set out to do the same for me as soon as time and circumstances permitted. I made it back just in time for the funeral.

The services were beautiful. The most difficult thing about the funerary process was watching everyone close to me grieve her loss so deeply. Of course, I was grieving too, but not because I felt I had "lost" her; I didn't feel that way at all. When last the two of us spent time together, she somehow knew that we probably would not have another chance to meet again in this life. She wasn't worried or afraid. She was simply resolved to go into the hereafter with everything in proper order.

As I laid in bed that night after her services, I fell asleep thinking about my grandmother and wondering where she was. I don't know where the belief originated for me, but I had always felt that those we love stay with us after they pass, even if just for a little while. So, as if she were sitting next to me on the bed, I spoke aloud, telling her that I loved and missed her very much, and would give anything to hear from her. I drifted off to sleep with a heavy heart, but woke the next morning feeling as if I had been given exactly what I had asked for.

I don't normally recall much detail from whatever dreams materialize as I sleep, but the dream I had that night was, in my view, much more than an ordinary dream. I was back in the funeral home sitting on a chair just across the room from where her open casket rested. I was the only one there, marveling at how beautiful she looked. I put my head in my hands and began to cry when I heard her voice say, "Don't cry. I haven't left you." I looked up, and she was sitting in a chair next to me. Yet, at the same time, her body was still lying in the casket. I looked back and forth at both faces, confused. "This isn't possible, Grandma. You're dead." To which she replied, "Well, I'm right here, aren't I?" She smiled, reached up and wiped the tears from my face, and told me that if ever I needed her, she would be there.

I kept the details of this dream to myself for quite some time, but eventually shared it with my mother during a conversation we were having about Grandma and how different life had been without her. She looked puzzled and said, "How bizarre. I had the exact same dream." I had believed the dream was a visitation before talking with my mother about it, but having learned that she had experienced the same thing, I knew beyond a shadow of a doubt that it had not merely been a coincidence.

Something similar would occur months later when my grandfather put their house up for sale. After his wife passed, Grandpa could not bear to live there without her. My family back home in Utah was tasked with sorting through and packing everything; something I was grateful not to be a part of, living out of state. It afforded me the ability to retain my memory of the house as I had loved it, with everything in its place. Had I had the means to purchase the home and keep it in the family, I would have. It broke my heart to think that it would be lost to us. My grandmother took a great deal of pride in her home, and it showed. Not only had my childhood been shaped inside those walls, so had my father's and my siblings'. To this day, I have never been back.

Just before the house sold, I had a dream that I went to see it one last time. As I pulled up into the driveway and got out of my car, I walked to the entry located under the carport, which is where I normally always entered the house. My grandmother was waiting there, holding the screen door open for me. Again, I expressed my confusion at her being there as she had passed away. All she did was smile back at me. As we both walked down the hallway that led to the family room, I noticed that the house was completely empty.

"I'm sorry, Grandma," I said. "I know how much you love this house."

"It's just a house, April," she replied. "You will always have your memories. Now it's time for a new family to make memories of their own here."

She embraced me, told me she loved me, and the dream ended. I woke up feeling completely at ease over something that had previously brought me a great deal of heartache. I would always love that house, but she was right. My memories were worth far more than the structure they were attached to. No one could buy them or threaten to take them from me.

It can certainly be argued that the thoughts and feelings weighing heavily upon my mind could have manifested such dreams. I accept that as a possibility. However, they brought with them such a peace and sense of resolution that I truly believe my grandmother was reaching out to me in the most compassionate and least shocking way possible. It would be easier for me to accept the visitation in a dream than it would had she simply materialized right in front of me.

The dreams would not be the only experience I had with my grandmother's spirit. In what little time I had been able to spend with her after I had gotten married and moved away, she had repeatedly questioned me about when my husband and I were going to expand our family by having children. I was in no hurry, and wanted to wait at least a few years before considering it, but she insisted we get working on it so that she could be around to welcome another great-grandchild.

About a month after her funeral and having returned to San Diego, I became desperately ill. My first thought was that I'd gotten food poisoning, as I couldn't keep anything down. Days passed, and I was no closer to recovery than I had initially been, so I made an appointment with my doctor and thought I'd soon be feeling well again. I was mistaken. After running a series of tests, the doctor informed me that what I was experiencing was not a nasty case of food poisoning. I was pregnant. Within an hour of having learned *that* news, a sonogram also discovered that I was expecting twins. I called my family back home, in a state of shock. I was both thrilled and scared to death at the same time.

As I returned to my apartment that afternoon, I opened the door to step inside and was immediately hit with the strong scent of a familiar perfume. I instantly recognized it as the perfume my grandmother had often worn. I was not aware of its name, nor did I have any of my own that closely resembled that scent, so there wasn't any reasonable explanation for it. In that moment, I felt as though she had come to congratulate me. It was the closest thing to a hug that my grandmother could have given me, and the scent lingered for several hours before finally fading away. I often joke that she made it up to Heaven and forced the issue, not only sending me one little one, but two just to make her point that I needed to start a family.

Real Ghost Hunters

Being a military wife, moving had become a regular event. My husband had re-enlisted for an additional three years of service on Whidbey Island in Washington State when we learned that I was expecting twins. Shortly after their arrival, I remember sitting in my apartment tending to the babies with the television on in the background when a program caught my attention. *Real Ghost Hunters* featured several different individuals being interviewed about their research and experiences with the paranormal. It was the first program of its kind that I had seen and I was thrilled when a couple on the show were said to be the founders of the Utah Ghost Hunters Society. Chris and Nancy Peterson were enlisted to investigate the Brookdale Lodge hotel in Brookdale, California, reportedly haunted by the restless spirit of a little girl named Sarah, who drowned there in 1918.

During the show, several audio clips that the Petersons had captured during their investigation of the hotel were played. I couldn't believe what I was hearing. Nancy would ask a question or make a statement, and the voice of a little girl would respond to her. I had read about Electronic Voice Phenomenon (disembodied voices captured on devices capable of recording audio) but I had never heard an actual example until that moment. Electronic Voice Phenomenon (or EVP) is the most commonly captured "evidence" of the paranormal. As soon as the show ended, I got online to look up The Utah Ghost Hunters Society, and I contacted the Petersons directly.

Chris and I had several conversations by phone, not only concerning the nature of his work but also the possibility of his investigating my childhood home. Having been the individual who experienced the most phenomena, Chris insisted I be there for the investigation. If something was centering around or was attracted to me in particular, for whatever reason, it would be helpful to have me attend.

At this point, my mother was completely open to the idea. Her only hesitation was that I might not get my father's blessing to have the house investigated. He and I didn't often talk about my fascination with ghosts and those I believed frequented his house. In later discussions with my father, I learned that it wasn't his hesitance to believe in such things, it was more a matter of not wanting to be acutely aware of them. He was more comfortable turning a blind eye, and I had to respect that. If there were ghosts in his home, he didn't want to know about it.

I desperately wanted the investigation to take place. I thought it would be an important and validating experience for me, so I pressed my mother for permission. She agreed, but Chris and Nancy would have to come in during the day while my father was at work so that he would not be upset about it. He didn't need to know.

Everything went according to plan. The Petersons arrived with their audio recording equipment and for several hours we moved throughout the basement as a group, recorders rolling. Within minutes, Nancy was eliciting responses from individuals we could not see. None of them were particularly revealing as far as information was concerned, but there were voices captured on the tapes that did not belong to any of us in the room. A male voice in the downstairs office identified himself as "Eddie," but no information about why he was in the house or how long he had been there could be obtained. Something was happening in the house we could not explain, but it was happening, and I finally knew beyond a shadow of a doubt that everything I had been through had been real.

My relationship with the Petersons grew, and Chris agreed to take me under his wing and teach me what he knew about capturing optimal EVPs. As fascinating as still photography and video were with regard to the paranormal, I focused my attention more on the audio. After all, I wanted to learn something from the spirits I was connecting with. With EVP recording, I might be able to put the pieces of several puzzles together, even if what was captured consisted of nothing more than two or three words at a time. It was something. It was communication, and I wanted more of it.

I returned to Washington with more questions, but with the knowledge that I wasn't crazy. Once my husband's enlistment with the Navy had ended, we returned to Utah, and I was back to spending a great deal of time in my parents' home. I spent hours upon hours walking around the basement with a recorder. EVP was my focus and fascination, but I wanted a different experience in a different location. The perfect opportunity would quickly present itself.

The Haunting of Lehi Hospital

I've always been a bit skeptical of places that claimed to be haunted, especially if advertising it as such was a way for the location to generate more revenue. This is not to say that they don't often have a legitimate claim; I've just never been the type of person to simply take anyone else's word for it. Haunted attractions are a draw for many people, myself included, but in order to maintain interest, some resort to rigging the scene so visitors leave believing they got what they paid for.

When I heard that a local former hospital building had been turned into a Halloween attraction just a few miles from where I lived, and that it was allegedly haunted, I wanted access. My oldest sister Courtney and I set out one evening to visit the Lehi Hospital building in Lehi, Utah, and to hopefully inquire about possibly spending some time alone inside. When we arrived, we were greeted by a group of teenagers practicing their roles for the haunted house. Prior to stepping into the lobby, I switched on my analog recorder.

The Lehi Hospital Building prior to being torn down – Lehi, Utah

I asked if the owner or manager of the building were present, which he was not, but a couple of the kids working there had a lot of stories to relate about things they themselves had experienced in the building. Our conversation was abruptly cut short when Todd (the owner) arrived and demanded that my sister and I immediately vacate the premises. I didn't have time to explain to him why I was there, but I would later learn that he believed we might have been organizers from another Halloween attraction interested in seeing their set-up to steal ideas or sabotage his operation.

Upon arriving home, I listened to the audio I had recorded during my brief visit. I had to rewind the tape to be sure I had heard it correctly. Literally seconds before Todd had entered the building and thrown us out, a whispery female voice was recorded saying, "Get out quick! Haaaaa." The voice did not belong to anyone in the room, nor had any of us heard it in real time. It was as if a spirit in the hospital was alerting us to Todd's imminent arrival, and knew he wouldn't be pleased upon discovering strangers in his building.

I returned the next night specifically for the purpose of apologizing for my intrusion, and Todd was quite receptive once I was able to relate to him what my motives actually were. I brought along the recording from the previous evening and played it back for him. From then on, I had access to the building whenever I asked for it. Sometimes, my sister would accompany me on my little excursions, but it eventually became too much for her and she chose not to tag along with me anymore.

I spent many a night in that hospital, most often by myself. After Halloween, the external source of power was disconnected. None of the plumbing or original electrical components were still functioning. During its years of operation (1926-1967) it is estimated that nearly 4,000 deaths occurred within its walls. Was it really that much of a stretch to think a ghost or two might still be wandering around the old building?

With my limited personal experience, and only a digital camera and audio recorder in hand, I spent countless hours on all three floors, talking to the air and hoping that something unseen would respond. One evening, while sitting in what used to be the main operating room, I asked, "How many of you died in this room?" Within seconds, I recorded one of the most interesting EVPs I've ever gotten to date. "Wait, she thinks we're all dead!"

This simple statement floored me. How could someone who had passed on not realize that they were deceased? This person, whoever it was, heard me and had reacted to my question in an interesting and unexpected way. If it had been a residual presence (a sort of energetic imprint on the environment that simply repeats itself like an audio or video clip) it would not have reacted to me at all. I had become quite familiar with random events that played themselves out over and over again, such as stories of sailors on retired naval ships running around frantically as if a battle were still raging. You can't interact with this type of phenomenon because it isn't anything more than a memory set to repeat itself. Some researchers in the paranormal field would argue that residual hauntings are responsible for a majority of reported phenomena. In my experience, however, they have actually been the minority.

Nothing further was recorded in the operating room or the remainder of the hospital building that night, but that one response was enough to bring me back to try again just a few days later. In the section of the building where the original patient rooms had been, I walked into a room and sat on the bed. With my recorder running, I sat in silence without saying a word for nearly a half an hour. I decided I would rewind the tape while still sitting in the room, and I was once again surprised and delighted upon discovering that I had recorded yet another fantastic EVP. "Momma! Michael! Momma, Michael's dead!" In my head, I pictured a small boy frantically clinging to his mother, distraught over discovering his brother had passed away. Of course, I would never know if that were the case, but hearing the emotion in the voice I had recorded really touched me. Had Michael passed away in this very room? I sat and spoke, trying to elicit some sort of response, but received none. Weeks later when I revisited the room, I recorded a nearly identical EVP. It was then that I realized the hospital building was home to both residual phenomena as well as intelligent. This location was everything I had hoped it would be, and my fascination with it was further fueled by the many experiences I would go on to have there.

One afternoon, I had arrived at the hospital while Todd was working on fixing certain problem areas of the building. I knocked on the main entrance door, and after several minutes, a young, olive-skinned boy opened the door. I asked if Todd were there and he simply nodded his head and moved aside as I stepped into the foyer. After closing the door behind me, the boy walked down the hallway toward the chapel area, and out of my sight. I called out for Todd, who met me in the foyer a minute or so later.

"Who is the little boy you brought along with you today, Todd?" I asked.

"What little boy? There aren't any kids allowed in here. Too many things for them to hurt themselves with."

"A little boy opened the door for me. It was locked, so I knocked and he answered it."

Todd had not entered the hospital using the front entrance that morning. He had entered in the back of the building, so someone had to have unlocked the front door, but he shook it off as nothing he needed to concern himself with and went back to his repairs. I walked through the entire building looking for that little boy. There were only so many places he could be. I did not find him, nor did I ever see him again.

One of the most startling events occurred when I went into the hospital accompanied by Todd, Chris and Nancy Peterson, friend and fellow investigator Brian Whitesides, and a couple of local newspaper reporters. On the upper floor, in a room where many people had said they'd seen and heard strange things, all of us stood together talking quietly. After just a minute or two, Todd reported that he was not feeling very well and excused himself. He packed up and immediately left that evening, trusting me to lock up afterward, which I often did.

The atmosphere felt heavy, and none of us felt at ease in the room. With his camcorder rolling and set to Night Shot, Brian nervously asked me to take a look at what he was seeing on the display. He had the camcorder focused on an old original hospital mirror hanging on the wall on the far side of the room. The room was pitch black, and nothing could be seen without the help of the Night Shot setting, but on the screen a face became visible in the mirror. It materialized, faded, and materialized again at a different angle. All of us stood frozen, watching this face peer through the mirror as if it were a window for several minutes. When it ended, the reporters were sure we had faked the incident somehow and began examining the mirror, as well as the remainder of the room. They found no explanation because there hadn't been one; certainly not one manufactured by any of us.

A few one-word EVPs were captured as we continued to explore, but nothing else significant occurred that evening. The reporters left feeling as though they had witnessed their first legitimate apparition, but it would certainly not be the last time I saw something frightening in the hospital.

One early afternoon, my close friend James Boley and I were back in the room where the face had materialized in the mirror. It was still light out, so it wasn't completely dark in the building. As he and I stood there adjusting the equipment we had brought along, I glanced down a hallway and saw someone standing at the end of it, just beyond some black plastic sheeting that hung about three feet off the floor. As I stepped into the hallway to find out who was in the building with us, the individual turned to the right and vanished. The problem was, there was nothing to the right but a solid brick wall.

Seeing the apparition had unnerved me, but it paled in comparison to what would occur later that same evening. As James and I made our way slowly through the building, we decided to spend some time in the basement where two brick crematory ovens still stood. Just passed the ovens, at the far end of the large room, was a crawl space that had been dug out, providing another exit from the building. I stood at the entrance to the crawl space with James, talking with my recorder rolling as he took a few photographs. As I peered into the darkness underneath the building, a chill ran up my body from my feet to my neck... and then something made a loud hissing sound into my right ear. Moments later, I heard what sounded like hurried footsteps running through the basement toward the stairwell leading back up to the main floor. We gathered our equipment, packed up, and decided to call it a night.

Over time, as I returned to the hospital to investigate further, I began experiencing something I had never expected. In the beginning, it felt as though I were intruding. It was as uncomfortable as it was intriguing. But, after several months, not only had I become more comfortable among the not-so-empty hallways of the hospital, but the unseen residents seemed to become more at ease with my presence there as well. It was not at all uncommon for me to enter the building and record things like, "Hi, April!" or "Missed ya." Sometimes I even heard these sentiments without the help of my recorder. Whoever haunted the hospital recognized me, and I believe they began to trust that I wasn't there to do anything but spend time among them.

I found that the wide range of phenomena I was experiencing (both in my childhood home as well as the hospital) had only initially been frightening to me because I lacked understanding. Most of us grow up being taught that ghosts are the result of overactive imaginations and don't really exist. So, when we encounter something we're told is imaginary, we fear the reality of it. I remember being afraid. I remember that it took time to outgrow the need to carry that fear around with me, but I did outgrow it. I developed such an emotional attachment to the Lehi Hospital that I was devastated to learn years later (after having once again moved out of state) that it had been torn down. Friends and colleagues of mine in Utah knew how much that building meant to me, and it wasn't long after its demolition that I began to receive artifacts in the mail.

In the occasions I have since visited the site where the hospital once stood, I have come to the personal conclusion that while the structure may no longer be standing, the spirits I had come to know and appreciate more than likely still maintain some measure of attachment. If they no longer continue to "haunt" the site, I am inclined to believe they visit it from time to time. Perhaps I simply want to believe that so as not to lose my connection to *them*. Whatever the case may be, I am and will always remain grateful for the glimpses of the other side that they provided me.

My fascination with the paranormal certainly survived even if my favorite hunting ground no longer did. Little did I know at the time that my fascination would help shape my career.

The Atlantic Paranormal Society (TAPS)

In 2005, I happened upon a television show on the Sci-Fi cable network (now SyFy) called *Ghost Hunters*. It featured Jason Hawes and Grant Wilson as head of The Atlantic Paranormal Society (TAPS) based

First-year anniversary issue of TAPS Paramagazine

out of Rhode Island. Jason and Grant conducted investigations of residential and commercial properties that were allegedly experiencing paranormal phenomena. By day, they held down jobs as plumbers for Roto-Rooter, but by night, they were attempting to validate or debunk claims of supernatural activity. I was instantly hooked on the show, and began to emulate the techniques they implemented in my own pursuit of answers to what lay beyond the veil.

I never missed an episode of *Ghost Hunters*. It impressed me that the team would often find perfectly reasonable and natural explanations for various occurrences, and did not label every unusual event as paranormal. This was important to me, as I felt it was a more realistic approach to ghost research.

Not long after I began watching the show, I read online that TAPS had its own print magazine, and it often accepted articles from the general public for publication. I had never written an article before, but writing was not entirely foreign to me. Creative writing was something I had always loved, and by the time I was in high school, I had already published several poems in various journals and anthologies.

I wrote an article entitled "The Haunting of Lehi Hospital" and submitted it to the editor for consideration. I had not expected it would be accepted, but it was, and the article was published in the magazine's first-year anniversary edition. Shortly after the issue was released, I was asked to become a staff writer, an offer I was thrilled to accept. I wrote a recurring column entitled "Ghosthunting: State-by-State" where I would highlight well-known haunted locations throughout the country. Eventually, I'd go on to write several cover stories as well as becoming the magazine's customer service manager. I took on a great deal of responsibility with the job, but it was one I absolutely loved, and I excelled at it. I was writing and immersing myself in a subject that had become such an integral part of my life. I couldn't have been happier with the position.

In October of 2006, Jason and Grant were to appear at the UNIV-CON event at Penn State University sponsored by the Paranormal Research Society on campus (which would go on to have its own show on A&E called *Paranormal State*.) I was sent to the event as a representative of *TAPS Paramagazine*, and it would be there that I would meet Jason and Grant in person for the first time. As *Ghost Hunters* gained momentum, so too did their schedule for personal appearances at various events across the country, and I was most often there to assist Jason and Grant with merchandise sales for both the show and the magazine. These events afforded me the opportunity to visit some of America's most famous haunted locations, such as The Stanley Hotel in Estes Park, Colorado, The Queen Mary in Long Beach, California, Eastern State Penitentiary in Philadelphia, and many others.

Jason and Grant were not only my employers; they became my friends. I worked hard for them, and they appreciated it. As my responsibilities with the magazine grew, it became increasingly difficult to work remotely from Utah, and I was offered an in-office position, which would require a move to Rhode Island where TAPS was headquartered. My girls and I packed up and headed to the Northeast.

As time went by and other opportunities arose, I eventually made the decision to move to Dallas, Texas, where I continued to write for the magazine, but ultimately pursued building a business of my own. In 2008, my husband and I established The Paranormal Source, Inc., a non-profit research and education corporation. We assembled a team of individuals with like interests, and began conducting investigations of our own throughout Texas and in various other places throughout the country.

Our reputation for being knowledgeable and professional afforded us the opportunity to investigate places not many had been granted access to before us, such as the Branch Davidian compound in Waco and the "Walls" prison unit in Huntsville, which houses the state of Texas execution chamber. In 2009, during large-scale maintenance upgrades, the prestigious and famously haunted Driskill Hotel in Austin had shut down. Our team was extended an invitation to investigate. It had been the first time in decades they had ever shut their doors to customers, and the only time a paranormal team had been given free run of the entire hotel.

Professionally, things were going quite well. I was content with the time I was able to spend in such fascinating places, and with people who shared my enthusiasm for the paranormal.

-3-
When Divided We Stand

"We can easily forgive a child who is afraid of the dark;
the real tragedy of life is when men are afraid of the light."
Plato

The Paranormal Source became a well-oiled machine. We investigated dozens of locations, recorded endless hours of audio and video, and often had interesting data to show for it. We were able to capture and to share this data with the public via our website or in various articles that I was publishing in print and online. When I wasn't actively investigating, I was poring over books by the dozens, asking questions of my mentors, and constantly searching for ways to improve the research process.

As the success and popularity of *Ghost Hunters* rose, so too did the number of investigators all over the country. Teams sprung up everywhere, and more and more people were becoming vocal about their interest in the paranormal. Many appreciated that Jason, Grant, and their team first tried to find alternate explanations to phenomena before labeling them supernatural, while others criticized them for not taking a more spiritual approach to their investigations.

Whether they are loved or hated is really an insignificant issue. The fact is, the *Ghost Hunters* television series broke ground and brought paranormal investigating to the public's attention on a large scale. The show was responsible for making it socially acceptable for people to involve themselves in ghost hunting and it quickly became mainstream. It no longer needed to be a hidden hobby, and anyone who had an interest in ghosts could find opportunities to try and interact with them. No special qualifications were required. It also allowed those who believed they were experiencing phenomena in their homes and businesses to express concern and ask for help without shame or ridicule – all positive things in my view.

On the flip side of that coin, however, the negative side effects became blatantly apparent just as quickly. People were obviously more invested in the thrill associated with spirit interaction than they were in actually attempting to research and understand the phenomena. What was being gained? I grew agitated with the influx of people who spent little or no time at all reading up on history. They simply became imitations of the people they watched on television and then it became a game of who could score a reality show of their own. The media quickly became oversaturated with paranormal programming. Some of the shows that were developed were decent and entertaining, while others just seemed to make a mockery out of the genre. I began limiting the amount of paranormal television I watched because I just couldn't stomach witnessing the downward spiral.

I had no interest in being on television. I didn't care about becoming a celebrity in the paranormal community because I wasn't in it to try and impress anyone. All I wanted – all I truly desired – was to experience what I could of the other side (without actually being there), to share those experiences with others, and hopefully help open up a few closed minds. I'd worked my way through and out of my fears about death and I sincerely wanted to help others do the same.

The community was comfortable existing as it was, and trying to get people to think outside of the box was nearly impossible. If a richer experience could be had, if just a little more knowledge about the other side were waiting to be obtained, why weren't more people reaching for it?

The whole thing seemed to evolve into one big popularity contest, and I wanted no part of it. There were too many individuals calling for unity among investigators, and yet actively tearing each other down over their differences in process, evidence, and whatever else they could find fault in with one another. Groups were laying claim to certain locations they'd investigated and berating anyone who attempted to gain access to them, as if to say, *Hey, these are our ghosts and they only come out to talk to* **us.** *Stay in your own yard.*

The drama was emotionally draining, and I was no longer finding inspiration to move forward among many in the paranormal community. While I didn't fully disappear, I scaled back my involvement with most events and limited my personal and professional affiliations to a smaller number of people. It wasn't that I was some sort of elitist; I just grew tired of the drama.

Investigations also became less and less important to me. I had experienced a measure of success with capturing clear and interesting EVPs, but I began to feel as though they weren't really providing me with any enlightening information. What was I learning that I didn't already know? I didn't have to prove to myself that ghosts existed, because they'd always been a real and present part of my life. I felt an overwhelming sense that I'd taken the research as far as I could. Friend and mentor Rosemary Ellen Guiley often referred to investigations throughout the community as "hamster wheel ghost hunting," and I was beginning to see her point. I wanted off of the hamster wheel while most others seemed content to keep repeating the same patterns.

I needed a new experience, one that could possibly point me in the right direction for progression. I had never personally spoken to or worked with a psychic before, as my pre-conceived notion was that they were probably all frauds or over-the-top personalities to whom you paid an exorbitant amount of money to speak to over the phone. I decided that if I were going to form any sort of opinion on psychics – whether good or bad – I should probably experience what they had to offer.

-4-
The Psychic Connection

"...Anyone who chooses to refer to psychic phenomena as superstition simply isn't aware of what's going in the world."
Richard Matheson

When traveling around to different events, I was often introduced to self-proclaimed psychics. Most of them were kind enough, and they didn't set off any alarm bells in my head, but I hadn't been "read" by one to really know one way or the other if the talents they claimed to possess were genuine or manufactured in order to make a living. I made no judgments; I just didn't have any experience.

The paranormal community was chock-full of psychics, empaths, sensitives, etc. Whatever you wanted to call them, their numbers swelled every time I crawled out of my cave to attend different functions. Every team seemed to have one (or more) and those that didn't showed little to no respect for those that did. No one could agree on whether or not psychics were a valuable asset to paranormal research or if they turned it into a carnival sideshow. I was looking to form my own opinion, rather than simply adopt the views of others.

I was first introduced to psychic medium C.J. Sellers while listening to a paranormal podcast on which she was the featured guest. Her warmth and sincerity were immediately endearing. The radio host offered to connect anyone listening with C.J. for a short on-air reading, and I took him up on that offer. I called in, but did not expect to be the caller chosen for the reading. C.J. and I were strangers to one another, and I wasn't prepared with any particular question to ask her. I introduced myself, and after a brief exchange of small talk she began.

Psychic Medium C.J. Sellers

"Your grandmother. An 'M' name? Is she your father's mother?" she asked.

"My grandmother on my father's side's name does begin with an M, yes," I replied.

I did not state her full name, nor did I share the information with C.J. that my grandmother was deceased.

"She's passed, but she comes through really strongly for you."

I was intrigued, but I was not yet sold on the authenticity of the experience.

"Madeline? No... is her name Marilyn?"

"Yes," I replied, a bit stunned.

"Well, she certainly has a lot to say, but I'm not comfortable sharing this information on the air. Would you have time to allow a private reading sometime soon?"

I was a bit disappointed that the reading had not progressed any further, but I also felt relieved that I would have time to delve further into this without an audience listening in.

C.J. and I connected a couple of days later via telephone, and the information she passed on to me was indeed quite private. In meticulous detail, C.J. described several recent events in my life and expressed concern for how I was handling them. I was careful not to give her information that could be used to make generalizations, but what she said to me could not have simply been guessed. An hour passed, and when it was time for us to end the call, I was left with several pages of notes I'd written about the messages she had been receiving on my behalf. Every one of them resonated.

In the years that have passed since that experience, I've had several additional readings with C.J., and have grown to consider her one of my closest friends and confidantes. When the time came to put together information for this book, and about psychic mediumship specifically, she was the natural choice to include for reference.

A Unique Psychic

C.J. Sellers first began providing readings for her close friends over fifteen years ago. She is clairsentient (able to clearly feel and identify an external emotion), clairaudient (able to hear the voices of spirits), and clairvoyant (able to see images outside of normal perception.) Every psychic is different, and does not always possess the same number of abilities.

As word of mouth spread about her gifts, she found herself reading for more and more people as time went on. Her client list today contains individuals from all walks of life. What sets her apart from many other individuals providing the same services might surprise you.

Her readings are guaranteed. No, she does not guarantee her clients that she will be able to connect with a specific loved one on their behalf. In the event that she is unable to psychically connect, or if the individual is displeased with the quality of information that is relayed during their reading, there is no cost. Her fees are modest and fair – unlike many of the "celebrity" psychics you see portrayed on television – and she is undeniably humble. In the dialogue that follows, C.J. and I discuss how people should be cautious when attempting to make a spiritual connection with the assistance of a psychic, how she sees the afterlife, and how the living are able to interact with it.

The Business of Being Psychic

"As a psychic, I imagine you come under fire for charging people a fee to connect with the spirits of those they've lost," I said. "How do you react to that?"

"Most people have been really good about this, because they understand it involves an exchange of energy. Unless you do this work, you don't really get it, but readings are exhausting; mentally, emotionally, in every way. The person receiving the reading generally walks away feeling better while the psychic feels drained. There is an awful lot of effort put into the process.

"I would challenge anyone to do what they do for a living – no matter what that is – and not get anything out of it. How long would they continue to do it? I don't care if you're a lawyer, a doctor, or a farmer; you have to be able to survive. This can be said of any profession. Now, if someone is charging an exorbitant amount of money, that's a totally different story.

"There are certainly those who claim to be psychic that aren't, who prey on the emotional instability of those experiencing immense grief in search of profit," I said. "To me, it takes a certain kind of evil to cheat and manipulate the bereaved. Finding a reputable and ethical psychic is probably quite difficult."

"If someone is looking for a psychic, the best advice I can give them is to talk to their friends. Talk to people that you know because word of mouth carries a lot of weight. If an individual is a good medium, they're going to have a long list of references. Clients should have the option of contacting them. Anyone can claim to have particular abilities, but speaking to people they've worked with is always your best bet as far as finding out how reliable they are. Also, it is wise to examine those the psychic is associated with. It is all in the company they keep."

"Skeptics often claim that what is happening between the client and the supposed psychic is nothing more than cold reading, which is stating overall generalizations that could apply to anyone and that have no real personal value." I said. "How can an individual identify whether or not they are being given this type of reading?"

"When messages are coming through that could apply to anybody in pretty much any circumstance, chances are they are receiving a cold reading. I would advise anyone to be cautious of what information or clues they themselves are giving to the psychic. If a client tears up during a session, a reader can say, 'I'm sensing you're very upset at the moment.' Anyone could sense that! What happens with readers who work this way is that they are not going to be able to give you details that really stand out to you; things that they couldn't possibly know or guess. If solid validations don't come through in a reading, chances are you are not dealing with the real thing.

"You also have to remain cautious of those readers who are arrogant or pushy about information. If they provide certain details to a client, and that client says, 'That doesn't really apply or make sense to me,' they should not react in a negative way and attempt to make that client feel stupid because the information is confusing to them.

"A good psychic should approach every reading feeling as though they are walking the plank. They should always be nervous about the quality of information that they're going to give out, because even with special abilities, they're still human. I believe that when psychics become overly confidant, they're going to be humbled by spirit. Ego can really muddy the whole experience."

Psychic Junkies

"I've seen people who often go from psychic to psychic, or repeatedly schedule readings with the same one because the information they've been given hasn't provided the exact sort of resolution they'd been looking for. Have you ever had a case where an individual has come to you for a reading, and kept coming back?" I asked.

"I haven't had too many experiences with people like that. I have a personal rule with my clients. I usually ask them to wait 3 to 6 months between readings, unless something major and life-changing happens and they feel they really need some guidance. If they are experiencing a great deal of grief they are finding difficult to process, I suggest counseling. If they are willing to see a therapist or a member of their religious clergy for help, I am willing to give readings right along with that. Counseling is the priority, not the reading.

"If someone is coming to me with the same question over and over again, or they're getting upset because the other side is giving them an answer they don't want to receive, I don't charge them and I send them on their way.

"There have been instances where I've had people get angry with me, and even lie to me. One of the first questions I ask my clients is if they've ever had a reading done before. I may not know how many readings an individual has had, but the other side certainly does, and that information can and does come out."

I shared with C.J. my opinion that it is precisely these types of individuals who give psychics a bad reputation overall. Psychic junkies, as I call them, are never satisfied and rely too heavily on the other side to solve their problems for them. When that is not done, they tend to want to blame the medium through which the messages were passed. Not every psychic is on the up-and-up, but remember, neither is every inquisitive person who seeks to have a reading done.

Interaction with the Afterlife

"Heaven is not a far off place," she began. "It is a place that exists right above our heads. There are those who, when they die, choose to remain earthbound, and it is not a psychic's job to assume they can tell that individual what to do. It's not like we can take their hand and say, 'Here, let me help you jump that fence.' All you can do is to tell them they have people they love on the other side that waiting for them, and allow them to make the decision on whether or not to move on."

"If they choose to move on, are the living still able to connect with them?" I asked.

"Just because they cross over, it does not mean that they can no longer communicate or spend time around their living loved ones. They can still visit the places they enjoyed spending time in while alive. They have the freedom to come and go as they please."

"When someone we know and love dies, people tend to encourage one another to let go or to somehow find closure with their death," I said. "But I don't think letting go is necessary. I just believe that the relationship changes."

"Absolutely," she agreed. "The relationship changes for both parties. I believe the person that has passed on also goes through a grieving process of being physically away from their loved ones. It's a two-way street. I do, however, believe it is a bit easier for those on the other side because they still see us, and can understand how the process really works. They are not physically limited like we are."

"Love never fails. It is the bond that never ceases to exist. In order to disconnect or truly let go of a person, you'd have to stop loving them, and you can't do that. They are spiritually always with you. It's their physicality that you have to let go of, but they haven't disappeared."

"You have to be willing to accept the loss," she continued. "We can't talk to those on the other side on a daily basis like we can while they're here. We're not meant to. You're also not going to physically feel them with you all the time. It happens on occasion, but only in times when we really need it. If we're constantly asking them to be with us and talk to us, we're not being fair to ourselves and we're not being fair to them. There is a reason why there is a separation between the realms. We are granted glimpses of the afterlife every once in awhile, but we've got to learn how to keep moving forward until it is our time to go and be reunited with our loved ones again."

The Search Continues

A lot of people hold fairly skeptical views on psychics, and honestly, I don't blame them. So many claim to be psychic, and so few actually are, but that doesn't detract from the value of the truly gifted. With any God-given talent (which I absolutely believe genuine mediumship is) it takes time for an individual to recognize, practice, and fine-tune their abilities. No one walks into something and is immediately perfect at it. I admire the sensitives who not only handle the skepticism of others with grace, but who do not allow criticism to deter them from doing the work they do. C.J. provided me with a measure of comfort I had not yet discovered in any other method of spirit communication at the time. I am grateful to have found her.

Naturally, even after a handful of psychic readings, I was still curious about different ways one could talk to the dead. While I was satisfied with the messages I'd received with C.J., I knew there were other methods to be researched that were just as controversial. I felt a desire to learn about and experiment with them.

-5-
The Dreaded Ouija

"As an interface between the worlds, the Ouija is neutral-neither good nor evil. The experiences that people have with the board depend on them and how they use it."
Rosemary Ellen Guiley

Growing up among ghosts was terrifying enough. The stories I would often hear from friends or family members about their personal experiences with Ouija boards only exacerbated my ever-growing fear. The Ouija board was a sure-fire way to open up the gates of Hell and invite all manner of evil and demonic forces into your life. Nothing good could come from fooling around with it. Nothing ever did, as far as anyone could tell me.

Long before I became aware of other tools and methods used for divination, the Ouija was the only way I'd ever heard of that could allegedly enable spirits to communicate with the living. It had such a stigma attached to it that I never thought I'd be brave enough to try using one. The negativity surrounding the board only intensified for me after having been frightened out of my mind by the media.

Let's revisit for a moment the all-too-familiar image of actress Linda Blair as she appears as a girl possessed by demonic forces in the 1973 horror classic, *The Exorcist*. Since its debut, the film has raked in over $400 million, captivating its audience with vivid and disturbing imagery of the battle between good and evil. The film, based on the 1971 best-selling novel by William Peter Blatty, tells the story of a young girl who establishes a connection through a Ouija board with an entity identifying itself as "Captain Howdy." Despite having a name that sounds like the host of a nineteen-fifties children's TV show, Captain Howdy turns out to have a sinister agenda, and the girl is ultimately possessed.

The first time I saw the film, I was convinced – not unlike the majority of others who saw it – that Ouija boards were bad news. I vowed

I'd never go near one, let alone try to make contact with a spirit through its use. I knew nothing of the board's actual history at the time, but in keeping with my desire to remove fear from the things I did not understand, I went in search of more thorough and accurate information.

The History of the Ouija Board

During the heyday of the Spiritualist movement in the middle nineteenth century, spirit mediums were regularly conducting séances for those who wanted to make contact with the other side. Ordinary people who possessed no psychic abilities also wanted to try and get in touch with the spirits. They formed what were called "home circles." These were groups of friends and neighbors who experimented with table tipping, knocking and rapping in reply to questions that were posed to the spirit world. Soon, they began looking for more efficient ways to contact the dead.

In 1853, a French educator who went by the pen name of Allen Kardec attended a séance where the participants used a little basket with a pencil attached to receive written messages from the spirit world. Kardec was so impressed by this new method of contacting spirits, which was far less time-consuming than calling out letters of the alphabet and waiting for rapped responses, that he made a note of it in his journal. Soon afterwards, the little baskets were replaced with a device called a planchette, a French word meaning "little plank." The first planchettes were small, heart-shaped pieces of wood with three little wheels on the bottom. The point of the heart held a downward-facing pencil. The idea was for a medium to place his or her hand on the planchette and then the pencil would write out messages from the spirit controlling the medium. This method of receiving spirit communications soon became a sensation in Europe. American tourists who were interested in Spiritualism brought back planchettes from their trips abroad. Word spread of their remarkable results and by 1868, when the planchette became widely available in America, thousands were sold. The invention was often used by mediums as a more elaborate form of automatic writing, but it really did not hold a wide appeal for use by general public.

A short time later, though, another invention came along that could be used by anyone. No experience was required and no real psychic skills were needed. This new device would revolutionize the Spiritualist movement and have an impact that still resounds today. The "talking board" – better known by its trademark name as the "Ouija board" – was born.

Legend has it that shortly after the planchette came to America, a cabinet and coffin maker from Maryland named E.C. Reichie created a new method of communicating with the dead. He devised a wooden lap tray with the letters of the alphabet arranged in two lines across the center of the board. Below these letters, he placed the numbers 1-10 and the words YES and NO in each lower corner. He used the planchette with his board but removed the pencil tip and the wheels and placed wooden pegs on the bottom of it. In this way, the planchette was free to move about the board.

It was said that Reichie named his board the "Ouija" because the name represented the French and German words for "yes" (*oui* and *ja*), however, legend has it that he believed that the word "Ouija" (which came to him through his talking board) was actually the Egyptian word for "luck." Suffice it to say, it's not, but wherever it came from, the name stuck.

The history of how the Ouija board became such a part of our culture is not as mysterious as strange messages from the other side, but it

does have a number of unusual elements to it. It actually took seven men, from very different backgrounds, to create the first mass-produced American talking boards. Those men were Charles Kennard, Harry Welles Rusk, Colonel Washington Bowie, Elijah J. Bond, William H. A. Maupin, William Fuld and the elusive E.C. Reichie (a man about whom almost nothing is known and who may not have existed at all!) These men pooled their assets, cash and resources to create the Kennard Novelty Co. of Baltimore, Maryland. All of the men had two things in common: Each of was a wealthy entrepreneur who was not opposed to taking risks and all of them were Freemasons. It is believed that they met through their association with this secret society and they soon made a pact to start the company.

Colonel Bowie initially handled most of the matters involving the company. Rusk was named as president, as he had the most experience with patent law and was able to file all of the necessary papers himself. Kennard owned some land and buildings from a defunct fertilizer company and he offered this property, located at 220 South Charles Street in Baltimore, for use by the new firm. Because of this, his name was used on the masthead. Elijah Bond contributed little to the firm, save for some ideas, and shortly after the patents were filed, he disappeared.

William Maupin remains a mystery to this day. He was gone before the company even got started and the only proof that he even existed at all was his name on the patent filings. The most active investor in the company was a young varnisher named William Fuld. He played a major role in the daily operations of the company, including production, and had many ideas of his own. Due to his age and lack of finances, when compared to the other investors, he had to work much harder to achieve success. It took him nearly a year to begin his climb to the top.

Historically, William Fuld has been acknowledged as the inventor of the Ouija Board, a fact that is confirmed by his descendants and those of Colonel Bowie. At the time the company was created, Fuld had little money to invest, but it is believed the idea for the board became his contribution, thus earning him a partnership and his name on the patent papers. He remains the name most connected to the boards today, despite the apocryphal legends of E.C. Reichie.

By 1891, the Ouija board was selling well, and on November 10 of that year, Charles Kennard filed a patent that would improve the performance of the board's planchette. This turned out to be his last act as a member of the Kennard Novelty Co. and one day later, he was removed from the board of directors. Although the company bore his name and used his land, Kennard was said to have been a poor businessman and so he was voted out. Years later, his descendants would claim that William Fuld drove Kennard out of business, but most likely it was Colonel Bowie. By 1892, Kennard was no longer listed in connection with the company but Bowie was named as manager and Fuld as supervisor. The company was moved to 909 East Pratt Street and the name was changed to the Ouija Novelty Company.

Soon after, Kennard tried to sell another version of the talking board that he called the "Volo." Bowie and Fuld responded by purchasing the Espirito trademark from the well-known W.S. Reed Toy Company. They placed an exact copy of the Kennard's Volo design on the back of their Ouija boards. Consumers loved getting two boards for the price of one and soon, Kennard's business was destroyed. He had no trademark for the Volo, so he tried to advertise the "Igili – the marvelous talking board" instead. It also failed and Kennard would vanish from the scene until 1919.

In 1894, the Ouija Novelty Co. moved to larger quarters at 20 North High Street, thanks to the fact that they were turning out huge numbers of talking boards. Bowie remained in charge of the company with Fuld and

Rusk as his side. A few years later, Bowie's other business interests caused him to sell out his share of the patents and he and Rusk both stepped into the background of the company. Production was turned over to Fuld, although Bowie would remain a financial part of the company for another twenty years.

Fuld now needed a partner. He had a day job as a customs inspector and was unable to devote himself full-time to the Ouija business. In 1898, he and his brother, Isaac, went into business together and they leased the rights to make the Ouija Board from Colonel Bowie. They split the proceeds from the talking board production and from other games. By April 1901, though, the partnership was over. William and Isaac had a falling out and Isaac was fired. The two of them never spoke to one another again, except in court. Colonel Bowie employed his son, Washington Bowie, Jr., to represent William Fuld against his brother. The brothers returned to court again and again over the years, bickering about money, rights and even who had the authority to open any mail that was addressed to the company. This would be just one of the relationships that was utterly destroyed over what most people claim is just a game.

Fuld soon changed the name of the company to the William Fuld Manufacturing Co. and moved the Ouija business to 1208 Federal Street. Business started to slow down and from 1905 to 1907, Fuld moved the company into his home at 1306 North Central Avenue. By 1908, business had improved once more and he relocated to 331 North Gay Street and then on to 1226-1228 North Central Avenue. This building would remain the home of the Ouija until an enormous sales boom in 1919.

Meanwhile, Isaac Fuld was breaking an injunction that had been filed against him in 1901 by sending out samples of a talking board that he had created called the Oriole board. They were exact duplicate of the Ouija board, with the "Ouija" logo replaced with "Oriole." He named his toy business the Southern Toy Co. and operated it from his home.

At this same time, William decided to expand his company and issued press releases that stated that he was preparing for "big business." He took a risk and moved his company to an enormous, three-story building. The gamble paid off and Ouija board sales began to climb. This made 1919 perhaps the greatest year in the history of the company. Not only did William enjoy an income from national sales of the boards, he also began to see national acclaim. The remaining rights to the boards were assigned to him by Colonel Bowie, which only served to stir up the ongoing feud with his brother. The battle was soon to come to an end, however.

In April of that year, William began mailing letters to stores who placed orders for Isaac's Oriole board. He warned them that the boards violated his patents and anyone who bought them was breaking the law. When Isaac found out about the letters, he filed suit against William. But William countered with the allegation that Isaac had violated the injunctions filed against him in 1901. Isaac's case was dismissed and the judge ruled that he had copied and distributed the Oriole boards in violation of the injunction. A review of the trademark that he had filed revealed that it had nothing to do with a talking board – it was for a pool table instead. Isaac was ordered to pay all of the courts costs associated with the case and to never make another talking board.

Once the court battles were behind him, William continued to expand. He retired from his customs position to dedicate more of his time to the Ouija business. He later served in the General Assembly in 1924. Washington Bowie, Jr. continued as his legal counsel and years later, Bowie's son would recall his father sitting down with all of the children to look through toy catalogs. They were instructed to circle any boards that might infringe on the Ouija trademarks, and he recalled finding many of them. Bowie aggressively pursued each of them and strangely, never accepted any payment for this service.

In 1920, another talking board company appeared in the news. The Baltimore Talking Board Co. was started by two men named Charles Cahn and Gilbert Michael and they had absolutely no contact with Fuld or his business. They did, however, pay a fee to call their boards Ouija. The Internal Revenue Service collected tax on their Ouija boards in 1920, but the Baltimore Talking Board Co. resisted the tax payments, claiming that the boards were not as game but a spiritual tool, and therefore should not be taxed. They took the IRS to court and mysteriously, they were represented by Washington Bowie, Jr. in the proceedings. They lost and Ouija boards were considered taxable. They appealed the decision all of the way to the U.S. Supreme Court, but the case was never heard. Talking boards are considered taxable – and legally not a tool to communicate with spirits—to this day.

From 1919 to 1927, William Fuld continued to expand his business, offering cheaper forms of his board in an effort to combat knock-offs. He also sold a line of Ouija jewelry and even Ouija oil for rheumatism. He trademarked the Ouija board as the Egyptian Luck Board, the Mystifying Oracle and the Hindu Luck Board. Things didn't seem like they could get any better for him, but then on February 24, 1927, disaster struck the Fuld family. William always supervised any work that was done on the factory and when a flagpole needed to be affixed to the top of the three-story building, Fuld joined the workmen. When an iron support that he was leaning on collapsed, he fell backwards off the structure. He caught himself for a moment on one of the factory window ledges, but the force of his fall slammed the window shut and he plunged to his doom. Amazingly, the fall only left Fuld with a concussion and some minor broken bones. He would have recovered if one of his broken ribs hadn't pierced his heart on the way to the hospital.

William Fuld's children took over the company. Catherine and William A. Fuld ran the company until the youngest brother, Hubert, became president in 1942. Sales sagged for years but the talking board industry saw a renewed interest in the 1940s, around the same time that the Spiritualist movement enjoyed a brief revival, likely due to grief-stricken relatives of servicemen killed in World War II hoping to contact their lost loved ones. World War I and the Influenza pandemic of 1918-1919 accounted for a similar surge in sales. Many companies introduced their own talking board designs, offering extravagant designs and colors, but eventually, disinterest and a declining market saw each of the companies collapse to the Fulds.

The heirs maintained the company until 1966, when they sold out to Parker Brothers. Hasbro Inc. purchased Parker Brothers in 1991 and now owns all of the rights and trademarks to the "talking board" which they still produce in large numbers, including a pink Ouija board designed to appeal to little girls. In spite of the fact that it is now sold in toy stores, it remains an exact duplicate (albeit a more cheaply made one) of the talking board that was sold many years ago.

Ouija with Rosemary

Believe it or not, my first experience with a Ouija board wouldn't happen until after I'd turned thirty. I'd never owned one, nor had I ever seen one up close. My only knowledge of them came from the stories passed on to me by others, or by portrayals of them in the media. A Ouija board would eventually fall into my possession (pun intended) at a Christmas party gift

Rosemary Ellen Guiley

exchange. It was the glow-in-the-dark version, which is widely available for purchase in stores and online.

To be honest, I wasn't thrilled with the gift, but I brought it home and tucked it away in my bedroom closet with absolutely no intention of ever opening the box. Had it made its way into my hands at an earlier time in my life, I have no doubt that I would have been unnerved enough to immediately dispose of it without even the slightest hesitation. But, having been involved in studying the supernatural for quite some time at that point, I thought there would be no harm in allowing it to collect dust in my closet.

Months later, when my friend and mentor Rosemary Ellen Guiley traveled to Texas for a visit, we discussed at length the negative perception many people had of the board. I admitted that I'd never actually tried to communicate with the deceased using a talking board of any kind, but I had the commercial version sitting in my closet. Rosemary offered to be the second sitter (as two are generally required) if I wanted to experience it for myself. She's had many years of experience with most all methods of spirit communication. Who better to attempt a connection to the other side with if not her?

I will admit that I was disappointed in what occurred.... a whole lot of nothing. The experience was entirely anticlimactic. Don't get me wrong, I believe Ouija boards have the ability to connect the living with the dead (and other entities as well) but it was not successful for me. Perhaps it was because I had spent a healthy majority of my adult life shedding the thoughts, opinions, and passed-along fears of others where the board was concerned. It didn't work for me because I did not expect it to. I was not afraid of what might occur. I certainly did not place my hands on the planchette thinking "Captain Howdy" or one of his friends would come through to terrorize us.

My subsequent attempts to use a Ouija have not been successful. For whatever reason, the boards do not seem to work for me. They are more symbolic for me than a tool I personally find useful in my work with spirit communication. This is not to say that I do not believe they can and do work for others; I certainly do. However, I think many approach the Ouija misinformed, uneducated, and unprepared for what can occur.

Tool vs. Intention

After spending years using various methods in attempting to speak to the dead, I began noticing a peculiar division in the paranormal community with regard to the Ouija. Some investigators were adamant that implementing the use of a board was against some sort of unwritten moral code that should not be challenged. Others thought it completely acceptable. What was common among both groups was their use of technical devices to gauge and document the presence of supernatural phenomena.

Individuals who sit down in front of a Ouija board more often than not ask the question, "Is there anybody out there who is willing to speak?" while waiting for the planchette to begin spelling out responses. Others, for example, sit in the dark holding an electromagnetic field meter called the K-II and ask the same question while waiting for a series of lights to flash in response.

There are two common problems here. The first is that the K-II meter (manufactured by K-II Enterprises) for example, was not initially devised or constructed with paranormal research in mind. In fact, most of the tools paranormal investigators use were not. On the manufacturer's website (www.kiienterprises.com) the description and usage information provided for the device reads as follows:

"Measure the EMF (Electromagnetic field) strength of every electrical device in your home, workplace or school; outdoor power lines, underground lines and even when you travel and shop for appliances. Health concerns about the negative effects of ELECTRO MAGNETIC FIELDS (EMF) from appliances, power lines, and home wiring have caused the U.S. Government to issue a warning to use "Prudent Avoidance" to help reduce your exposure to this risk. Since EMFs are everywhere it may be impossible to totally avoid them. The Safe Range K-II EMF Meter can help you measure these potentially harmful fields and determine the safe range to help reduce exposure. It also helps you determine which appliances produce high level emissions."

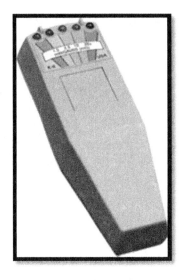

Paranormal investigators use the K-II on the theory that ghosts both manifest from and emit electromagnetic fields. Again, this is just a popular theory and has in no way been scientifically substantiated. Paranormal investigation is simply a combination of theory, personal perception and experience. So, why have we placed more faith in the K-II to validate our experiences and far less in the Ouija?

The second most common problem I have encountered is how blindly people physically and mentally open themselves up to whomever (and whatever) may be willing or desirous to communicate, especially when they're physically involved in the interaction by either holding a meter or placing their hands on a planchette. Any device that uses you as a medium should be handled with caution and treated with respect.

In her book *Ouija Gone Wild* with co-author Rick Fisher, Rosemary Ellen Guiley makes an excellent point:

"Spirit communication is a strange brew. It is unpredictable, and colored more by the living than the dead and discarnate. The availability of talking boards does not mean that the boards should be taken lightly in their potential to open interdimensional doors. If you were to travel to a foreign land, you would want to take some time to research it, its attractions, its safety, and its inhabitants. You would prepare yourself for the trip. People don't seem to think those considerations are necessary for traveling into the spirit realms."

If one is interested in attempting spirit communication using *any* method or device, acquiring knowledge about its history, how it works, and what the potential risks are is essential. As with any tool in an investigator's arsenal, it is most often the intention (and behavior) of the user that dictates the resulting experience when using it, and not the tool itself. Once you have a solid foundation of knowledge in place, you are far more likely to not only experience a legitimate connection, but it is also more likely to be a positive one.

-6-
The Ghost in the Box

"The more enlightened our houses are, the more their walls ooze ghosts."
Italo Calvino

Long, long ago in a laboratory in New Jersey, one of the preeminent minds of the 20th century pondered the possibility of communications with the dead. While Thomas Edison's fascination with this subject has been questioned in modern times, the man who gave incandescent light to the world, as well as the ability to record sound and motion pictures, seems incontrovertible. Whether his thoughts made it onto paper or if they survived his death is another matter, but anecdotal evidence seems to suggest that he, along with radio pioneer John Hayes Hammond, Jr., Alexander Graham Bell, Guglielmo Marconi and even Nikola Tesla all worked on this concept at one time or another.

While I could fill pages with the work of men like Hammond, a close personal friend and protégé of Edison, the actual creation of a working "telephone to the dead," only becomes well documented with the experiments of George W. Meek and the Meta Science Foundation, who created a series of communications devices later referred to as spirit communication devices or SPIRICOM. In all, there were five such devices, the Mark IV being their only real success. According to Raymond Bayless and D. Scott Rogo, both of whom were well-known paranormal investigators and experimenters in early Electronic Voice Phenomenon (EVP) research, the Mark IV succeeded in opening a two-way channel between the living and another reality. While the earliest of the EVP research was stumbled upon by accident when Frederick Jurgensen first reported recording voices while attempting to capture rare bird calls in

Europe, it was not until the Mark IV that anyone was successful in a dialogue with such disembodied speakers.

Recordings of some of these communications are still available on the internet and it is useful to note the difference between the earliest of these communications and later ones. The first Mark IV successes were with someone or something that sounds very robotic. The Mark IV device was housed in a series of cumbersome radio devices, reminiscent of early ham radio gear. It was neither portable nor easy to operate. Later devices were created, it is now reported, with the postmortem help of a former Cornell physics professor, Dr. Nick Mueller, who had died in 1967 and returned to collaborate on devices with Meek. Recordings of those collaborations are also still available. They are fascinating to listen to, but the voice and tone is again very mechanical.

As later devices were introduced other voices came through, but some of these "spirits" seemed to raise doubts among the more skeptical researchers. As an example, in one recording of a dialogue with someone reportedly contacted who apparently died in the 1830s, the "spirit" says "okay." This would be a problem historically because that word did not exist in anyone's lexicon during the reported spirit's lifetime. "OK" was a term coined by early railroad telegraph operators several decades later. Either the spirit had picked it up by listening to the researchers (which is entirely possible), or the contact needed more in-depth investigation. While we could nit-pick about the minutia of some of these exchanges, the concept seemed clear: Certain experimenters were somehow communicating with unknowns using non-traditional methods.

At this point, the subjects with whom the experimenters were talking could not always be clearly identified. The devices that followed found their way into several sub-sets of paranormal investigators including UFO experts, ghost hunters, psychics and those who were studying the possibility of the existence of multiple parallel universes.

No discussion of this subject would be complete without introducing the father of 'The Box,' Frank Sumption, a licensed ham radio operator and electronics technician who conceived of a truly universal radio receiver that would enable anyone to listen to these communicators and interact with them. Sumption's early efforts were, in his own words, aimed at creating a device that you could put on a table like any other radio to listen and communicate, much like a ham radio, except that rather than seeking to talk with someone in the next county or across the ocean, you could theoretically talk to the dead. Frank's box was a creation fashioned from components he had on hand in a spare parts box. What he didn't have on hand, he rescued from old discarded radios and TV sets, or purchased from Radio Shack.

Frank's first box stood apart from its predecessors in that it was aimed at utilizing the AM radio band and was much smaller than the bulky SPIRICOM devices. The box simply scanned the AM radio band, picking up bits and pieces of broadcasts and white noise. The end result was amazing – a box that could answer questions asked by the operator. Sumption has made many variations on the box. In fact, no two are exactly alike.

Frank's Box & the Stanley Hotel

By early 2007, I had begun hearing about the Frank's Box in various circles, and was admittedly intrigued with its reported potential to facilitate conversations with spirits in a way that I had not yet witnessed or attempted. While traveling to assist Jason Hawes and Grant Wilson during a Darkness Radio/TAPS event at the Stanley Hotel in Estes Park, Colorado, in March of that year, I learned that an individual by the name of Chris Moon would also be attending the event to demonstrate his use of the Frank's Box. Chris, a paranormal investigator and senior editor of *Haunted Times Magazine* was a friend of Sumption's and had been working with the devices for some time.

On the evening of the demonstration, numbered tickets were handed out that had been drawn at random. Those in possession of the correct numbers were given an opportunity to approach the Frank's Box and to ask to speak to a deceased individual of their choosing. Chris operated the device with the assistance of psychic Chip Coffey, who helped to decipher the resulting messages. A spirit control or "technician" on the other side was said to be assisting by bringing the spirits who had been requested to speak.

I stood quietly to the side, listening, grasping bits and pieces of what I could hear from where I stood. It was admittedly exhausting to listen to the constantly shifting and broken radio signals, but I tried my best to focus on anything that might be clear and relevant. Some exchanges were impressive, while others failed to yield anything of note.

At the time I was given my numbered ticket, I knew (although I do not know how) that my number would be among those called. It was. As I approached Chris and the Frank's Box, I was unsure of whom I would ask to speak to. When I was a child, I'd loved a family friend by the name of Nolan, who had become a sort of grandfather figure to me. It had been several years since his death from bone cancer, and he was the first person that came to mind. The situation was a bit uncomfortable for me, as I wasn't sure if I even believed it was possible to communicate with the deceased using such a device, let alone someone I'd personally known. I spoke Nolan's name, and waited for any sort of recognizable response.

I wish I could say that what occurred instantly convinced me of the box's potential, but it did not. I was only given a few minutes to attempt a connection, and I honestly cannot remember what if anything was said that would have led me to believe Nolan had been on the other end the line. I walked away from the experience with more questions, and the desire to not only have an opportunity to try again, but to own and operate a Frank's Box myself.

After returning from the event, I reached out to Frank Sumption via email and inquired as to what the likelihood of obtaining a box for my own research would be. Initially, he did not respond. I realized he must have been receiving requests from dozens of individuals, if not more. I did not take the lack of response personally, and for a short time, I left the issue alone.

As more and more information (and controversy) began to surface with regard to the boxes and their proper use, I found my interest in obtaining one renewed. The opinions of others did not deter or sway my own in either direction; I needed access and time with a box to determine what I personally thought of its use. When next I reached out to Frank, he replied that he was growing rather tired of people making such requests, and that my chances of obtaining one were slim to none.

Meanwhile, smaller, more easily obtainable radios were being altered by many in the paranormal community to work on the same basic principle as the Frank's Box. Certain portable models being sold through Radio Shack became the popular choice, and after having been altered, they were referred to as "Shack Hacks." I purchased a radio, had it altered to continually sweep the radio band, and set about testing it out. Sadly, despite my efforts, the Shack Hack proved itself useless to me.

Ron Ricketts & the MiniBox

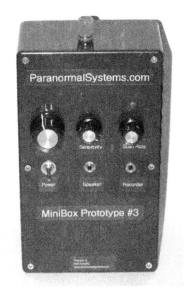

Original MiniBox

As the interest and demand for Frank's Boxes grew, so too did my frustration with my inability to obtain one. My work with EVP was consistent, and quite successful, but I felt driven to keep up the pursuit to work with the technology I'd only briefly been exposed to in Estes Park. Many discussions were had with friends and colleagues of various diverse backgrounds. One friend in particular, investigator Ron Ricketts, believed he could create a similar device of his own. Ron had an extensive professional history in electronics and engineering, and possessed the knowledge needed to map out a device and ultimately build it. After months of planning, the MiniBox was born.

Ron had designed and printed his own unique circuit boards, installed them along with the other necessary components in a smaller, more modern housing, and handed me a prototype. Not unlike the Frank's Box, the rate at which the device scanned the AM radio band could be manipulated, as could the sensitivity of the signal and volume at which sound was produced through an external speaker.

Shortly after having received the MiniBox prototype, I was to travel back to the Stanley Hotel for yet another paranormal event. Rosemary Ellen Guiley, Frank Sumption, and Mark Macy (a long-time authority on spirit communication) would all be in attendance as well. I knew it would be a unique opportunity not only to spend time with people whom I admired, but to personally introduce them to the MiniBox as well.

Both Rosemary and I took turns operating the device, which proved immediately impressive. At one point, while she and I were working with the MiniBox in my hotel room, it began clearly repeating the name "Mark Macy." Rosemary and I both concluded that whomever we were in touch with knew that Mark was close by and was, in a way, being summoned. When Mark was located, he was not at all surprised at the news he'd been requested, and accompanied us back to the room. This was one of many

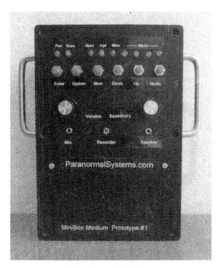

MiniBox Medium

incidents that would prove to me that those on the other side are acutely aware of what we are up to, and often have requests of their own.

The conversation I witnessed between Mark and the individual(s) he connected to rendered me nearly speechless. It wasn't simply bits of voices and music being mixed together to create responses. The radio noise continually shifted, yes, but one singular voice would carry over it without interruption for several seconds at a time, and the responses directly related to what Mark was saying. Overall, it was an experience that further inspired me to keep an open mind with regard to the relevance of such devices being used for research.

While this particular prototype of the MiniBox worked for me, I noticed that it worked far more consistently for Rosemary. I returned to Texas, spoke with Ron, and detailed for him the experiences we'd had working with the box. I expressed my opinion to him that if anyone were to own and operate that specific device, it should be Rosemary. He agreed, and I would hand deliver it to her when the next opportunity presented itself.

Ron built a prototype of the original MiniBox design for me shortly thereafter, along with an upgraded version he called the MiniBox Medium. The Medium had all the same functions as the original, but also included the addition of several different scanning modes, the ability to save a particular setting for repeated use, and handles that were directly hardwired to the internal components. This allowed the individual using the device to not only hold it in their hands, but to use their body to amplify the incoming signal just as an antenna would do.

Frank's Boxes #37, 38, and 73

There was a time when owning and working with a Frank's Box seemed quite impossible to me. I'd known through my correspondence

Frank's Box #73

Frank's Box #37

Frank's Box #38

with Frank Sumption that too many people were making requests (and often unwarranted demands) for him to provide them with boxes, and I did not want to be one of those people. Whenever I had a question, Frank was kind enough to respond, and the two of us maintained communication through email for quite some time.

I was both surprised and elated when Frank agreed to build devices for me to work with. All of Frank's boxes are numbered in the order they are built. I received #37, followed shortly thereafter by #38, and would be the eventual owner of #73. Two of the boxes—37 and 73—worked wonderfully for me. However, I was unable to obtain results with 38 and ownership of the device was eventually transferred to my friend and fellow investigator Marc Magsaysay, for whom it works quite consistently.

Testing, Testing, 1-2-3

The Frank's Boxes and MiniBox devices quickly became my sole focus in ITC research. The more I used them, the more I began to realize that it wasn't just a matter of turning on the boxes in haunted places and asking questions. There was a great deal to learn, and I was only going to figure out how it all worked by trial and error... and error... and error.

One evening, shortly after having received #37, my sister Courtney was visiting and asked if she might be able to witness how the device worked. As I powered it on, I asked if there were anyone in particular who had passed on that she'd like to try to reach.

"My friend, Beth," she said. "I don't really know what happened, but some are calling her death a suicide and others think she was drugged by her boyfriend."

I had spent time with Beth years earlier, and I knew the mysterious circumstances surrounding her death at the age of 23 troubled my sister deeply. I made it clear to Courtney that she should not expect a reply from Beth, but if one occurred, it could be an emotional shock.

We sat in silence for several minutes, letting the box cycle back and forth across the AM radio band. As I made adjustments to the scan rate and volume, I instructed Courtney to begin asking for her friend by name.

"But is there something I need to speak into?" she asked.

"No," I replied. "Spirits don't need the device in order to hear *us*. We need it in order to hear *them*. Just put your intention out there, and if she hears you, hopefully she'll try to talk to you."

For several minutes, Courtney called out to her friend Beth, with no recognizable response. Just as we were about to abandon the idea that she might be reached, a female voice clearly and distinctly yelled out, "Courtney!"

The look on my sister's face was of complete shock. She didn't respond until the voice repeated her name, almost in a panic.

"Beth, is that you? I... uh... is this actually working?" she asked.

"Yes! Yes!... working... Beth."

Tears began streaming down Courtney's face, and she admitted to me that she didn't know what to say to keep the conversation going. It was all a bit bizarre to her. I advised her to just talk to her friend the way she would if Beth were standing right there in the room with us.

"Are you okay?" she asked. "Can you tell me what happened to you?"
No response.
"Hello? Beth? Are you still there?"
No response.
"Beth, if you're really there and can hear me, please keep trying!"

74

"I'm here," said the voice. "Okay."

Courtney began expressing her concern over what had happened the day Beth had died, when she was interrupted in mid-sentence by the voice now blaringly clear coming from the box.

"Not a suicide!"

This same phrase was repeated a number of times, and the voice once again went silent.

"I love you Beth."

"Love you, Court."

My sister tried to ask several more questions, but we received no further response in the better part of the hour that we spent trying to keep the connection. As I switched the box off, Courtney hugged me and thanked me for providing her with the experience. While I had very little to do with it, I was pleased that it had given her the peace of mind I'd hoped it would.

With each new success I went on to have with the radio devices, my enthusiasm about them grew. Some found it odd or thought it unwise to be using them within the confines of my own home, but it seemed practical to me. Traveling to various locations to conduct trials seemed unnecessary and time-consuming. However, when opportunities presented themselves to test the boxes in reportedly haunted locations, I took them.

During one of my many visits to the Stanley Hotel for an event, I brought along the MiniBox prototype. A small group of individuals were granted access to the carriage house on the hotel property. It was not open to the public, it had been reported to be incredibly active, it was an invitation I was pleased to accept.

Upon entering the carriage house, it didn't take long for the group to begin seeing and hearing strange things. Most of us saw several figures materialize and approach us just to shrink and fade away moments later. The distinct sound of heavy footfalls on a wooden surface were heard by everyone, yet the wooden flooring in the carriage house had long since been removed and only dirt remained in the area of the building where the sound was heard. After a fascinating couple of hours had passed, I suggested experimenting with the MiniBox.

The radio signal in the area was weak due to the hotel's location in the mountains, and most of what emitted from the MiniBox was nothing more than static. Initially, I did not have much hope that it would work at all, but it did. I began asking questions about the slightly hostile feeling many of us sensed throughout the evening when a male voice pushed through the static.

"Run."

"No," I responded. "We're not going anywhere. Why would we need to run?"

"They're here... RUN."

These were not messages simply pieced together by random bits of radio noise, as we could hardly pick up a signal at all. Someone was urging us to leave, but as is often the case with me, I wanted to be presented with a justifiable reason to go.

"Who are 'they?' Are we in danger?" I asked.

"...Prey on your own..."

This statement garnered a collective gasp from the group, and then the box fell silent. I could elicit no further response from the disembodied speaker. Exhausted, and admittedly a little unnerved, the group decided to call it a night and head back up to the hotel. I look back on this particular incident and wish I'd have stayed to investigate further. Whoever "they" were, I'll likely never discover.

Personal Observations

Frank's Boxes are not widely available to the public. Each and every one of his devices is built by hand, and is unique in appearance, made with varying components. They are genuinely one of a kind. The MiniBox was eventually made available to the public. However, after having invested a large amount of time and money into the development and production of the boxes, Ron could not recover enough from sales to break even. He ultimately decided to discontinue manufacturing the MiniBox.

I consider myself extremely fortunate for having been given the opportunity to work with "ghost boxes" of all kinds. Investigators often ask my advice on how they might be able to obtain the coveted devices, and I am always at a loss for words. Beyond my initial interest in them, I haven't actively sought them out. The boxes, in their various forms, just seem to find their way to me. I've received all manner of devices from both public and anonymous sources. Frank Sumption, Ron Ricketts, Steve Hultay and others have all been generous in providing me with the technology.

It is because I have spent a great of time and energy working with the boxes that I have come to the personal conclusions that I have about them and their relevance in paranormal research and investigation. While these observations might not be set in stone, they have been consistently effective for me while working with the boxes over the past several years.

Observation #1— Owning a device does not guarantee it will readily function for its possessor. Obtaining one of the more desirable devices is only half the battle; getting it to work properly for you is a fight in and of itself. I do not yet know what sets one individual apart from another, but it has been my experience that the boxes work beautifully for some and not at all for others. It's a frustrating reality, but a reality nonetheless.

Observation #2— The boxes tend to produce results more consistently for the individual who works with them the most. Whatever energy is at work to allow the connection between the living and the dead to be made, that energy is sensitive and can easily be disrupted. The process of becoming familiar with a spirit communication device is something I refer to as "imprinting." Building a communication bridge between the physical and spiritual realms takes time and trust.

The boxes in my possession do not tend to work well when I hand them off to others to experiment with. I have tried to share the experience with many people in the field that I respect. Skeptics, believers, and those who walk the line in between have often used the devices on loan. Two things are immediately apparent upon their return. The first is that results are often lackluster (or non-existent) for the individuals that temporarily work with them. The second – a rather irritating complication – is that once I have them back, they consistently refuse to work for a lengthy period of time, even for me. In the beginning, I thought they were somehow physically damaged and needed repair, but upon closer inspection, nothing had been broken or out of place. Only after leaving the devices alone and unused for several weeks or months, would they begin functioning for me again.

I've concluded that at least to some degree, I have been punished for personally disconnecting, or for assuming I could loan something that wasn't in my power to loan. Make no mistake, I sincerely want others to experience the results I know these devices are capable of, and I have gone to great lengths to facilitate that, but in the end, it really isn't up to me. It has to be mentioned that even while certain friends and colleagues have been unable to obtain results on their own with the devices in my collection, many of them can and have attested to the fact that they've witnessed the devices working when I am the operator.

Observation #3— When the devices work, patience, respect, and a discerning mind are required in order for them to *continue* working. If you expect them to provide you with a lengthy conversational exchange every time you turn them on, I guarantee you will be disappointed. After all, the boxes are just tools; you cannot force spirits into communicating with you according to your timetable, nor can you engage them in conversation on subjects they have no desire to discuss. You can request to speak to a certain individual, but do not expect your request to be answered. Instead, be grateful when it is, and remain hopeful you'll have another chance in the future when it is not. The dead are no different from the living. Why do we assume we can make specific demands of them?

Observation #4— Spirits who become familiar with and comfortable speaking through a particular device will often follow it to different locations. Remember, ghosts are not physically limited. If you work with a ghost box at home, for example, and the voice of a departed relative happens to come through, you should not be surprised when that same voice speaks to you while you're sitting in the dark at some random haunted location during an investigation.

When I first began working with Frank's Box #37, all of my initial trials were conducted within my own home. The voice of a little girl frequently came through to speak with me. While I have never been given her name, her voice is unique and instantly recognizable. I was both surprised and overwhelmingly pleased when I traveled with the device to different locations and she continued to come through for me.

If the line is open, it is a mistake to assume the only people you are likely to hear from are those who've chosen to stick around a particular site.

Observation #5— It has often occurred to me that while I do not always receive a valid verbal response when operating the various pieces of equipment, it can still be a useful experience to keep them running. For whatever reason, just having them powered on has often resulted in a palpable shift in the immediate energetic environment, and other phenomena have manifested. It is not at all uncommon for the temperature in the room to change dramatically and without natural explanation. Knocking sounds are often heard moving about the room. When the signal for invitation is broadcast, it is often answered, but not always in the way one might expect.

Observation #6— Using ITC devices (or attempting communication with spirits (via any method) while in the midst of emotional distress is unwise. This is simply due to the law of attraction. Turmoil will more often than not attract attention from entities (or whatever your preferred label might be) who are less than honest, and who like to cause confusion and further upset. If you want to have a positive and uplifting spirit communication experience, it makes sense to attempt it with a positive and uplifting attitude.

Observation #7—A friend of mine recently said that he didn't trust the various spirit boxes because he did not believe one could be certain of just who or what was speaking through them. The dead have the ability to lie, of course. What if false information were being provided by someone claiming to be someone other than who they actually were? My response was that I often have the same problem with the living. I have no way of knowing if they really are who they portray themselves to be, or if what is going to come out of their mouths is the truth. I couldn't very well condemn the use of my telephone because I wasn't sure I could believe what was being said on the other end of the line. Trust your instincts, use common sense, keep your wits about you, and while I certainly can't guarantee your experience will be a truthful one, you will have at least learned that communication using the devices *is* possible.

Observation #8— When you want the connection or the experience as a whole to end, clearly state your intention, ask that you have your privacy and space respected, and power down. Many people in the paranormal community (especially those returning from an active investigation) worry that spirits will "attach" themselves and follow them home. Well, the truth is, they might follow you home if that is what they choose to do, but if you treat them with respect, it is my experience that they will repay you in kind. In asking a spirit to be on its way, I've never had to make the request twice.

-7-
Eleven Minutes

"So, even after I am gone, do not shut the door too tight,
in case I should want to come again, for I might have something
immensely important to say."
X, Letters From the Afterlife

Early on in my experimentation with ITC, I learned that opinions within the paranormal community widely varied with regard to which devices or methods provided the most consistent or authentic results. The individuals who claimed the Frank's Boxes (and other similar devices) worked were often deemed frauds by those saw them as nothing more than useless, broken radios. Oftentimes, these criticisms would come from people who had never actually sat down and invested any time working with the boxes, which I found peculiar, and honestly quite irritating.

The Frank's Box and Minibox devices did indeed work for me, and in a way that convinced me that it was possible to connect to the deceased through their use. "Broken radios" or not, they worked, and I didn't particularly care whether or not the skeptics believed me. This view that a ghost or spirit couldn't possibly communicate with us through something so simple was asinine to me. Why should spirit communication require something more complicated or high-tech? We have access to advanced technology, yes, but it doesn't mean it is always necessary or useful. The dead have been talking to us for centuries. The problem is on our end of the line; not theirs.

By late 2009, however, I was working with the boxes less and less. I had grown weary of listening to broken radio signals hoping for a two or three-second response that seemed worthwhile. What was I learning that I didn't already know? Nothing. As a child, my motivation to learn how to communicate with the other side was inspired by fear. Over the years, fear turned into fascination, and fascination evolved into a much greater need to know – and not just believe – that an afterlife existed. That need was satisfied, yet I still craved more knowledge about how it all worked.

I wasn't ungrateful. Every time the boxes worked (which again, was not 100 percent of the time) I expressed gratitude for the experience. But, no matter how grateful I was, I still felt disconnected, as if I were unable to grasp even half of the bigger picture. Discouragement settled in and I was beginning to believe I'd gone as far as I could with the research until I was contacted by an individual using a different type of ITC device.

Andy Coppock is a biomedical research scientist and laser physicist located in Los Angeles, California. When he and I first connected in early 2010, I had no previous knowledge of him or the paranormal research he was conducting. He had somehow come into possession of a piece of investigation equipment with my last name written on it, and sought to locate its owner, which lead him to me. After a few initial discussions, Andy was made aware that I was focusing a majority of my time on ITC research, and he wanted me to review an audio recording he had captured while using a device he called the "Probe." I knew nothing of the particulars of the device at that point, but I was directed to the audio that was set to a photo slideshow on the YouTube website. The video was several minutes long, and appeared to contain a conversation between Andy, his research partner, and a disincarnate entity named Charlie Deagan who was thought to haunt the now-closed Yorktown Memorial Hospital in Yorktown, Texas.

I knew right away that the device he was using to facilitate the conversation – even without being able to see it – was nothing like the ones I used, in that it was completely devoid of radio noise. There was, however, a fluctuating buzzing sound that seemed to grow louder whenever the alleged entity was speaking through it. Even with the interference, Charlie's responses were, for the most part, clear and concise. I didn't have to strain to hear what he was saying.

I played the video several times in succession, wanting to believe it was authentic, but I was plagued by doubt. I had never heard anything that impressive in all my years of working in both EVP and ITC research. I did not personally know Andy; we had only talked to one another via social media and email. I had no idea what the Probe looked like or how it functioned. Naturally, I flooded Andy's email inbox with questions, and he responded by saying that I might have the opportunity to see the device in action and in person fairly soon. He and his research partner, Michelle

Victoria's Black Swan Inn – San Antonio, Texas

Brown, often made trips to San Antonio to visit friends and hold events, and he would be happy to have me down to one to witness the phenomenon for myself.

The first scheduled event that I was invited to attend in March of 2010 was unexpectedly canceled, but another was set for October. Andy was to speak in front of a small group of investigators at Victoria's Black Swan Inn before conducting a live demonstration with the Probe. The Black Swan Inn is a private residence and event venue in San Antonio with a rich haunted history.

I cleared my schedule, made the necessary arrangements, and eagerly waited for the day to arrive. When it came, I had convinced myself to remain neutral and to objectively observe whatever might unfold before coming to any conclusions. I was going as a researcher, and not to be entertained.

In all, an estimated thirty or so individuals arrived for the event. While most of them were strangers to me, a handful of friends and colleagues from Washington State and Tennessee had made the trip in as well. I had no idea what to expect, and the events that unfolded over the course of the next two evenings would forever change my views on not only spirit communication and ITC research, but on life and death as well.

On the evening of October 8, Andy spoke to the group at the inn about the various experiences he had had while developing and using the Probe. He related to the group that he often had the assistance of what is historically referred to as a "spirit control," which is an individual on the other side who assists in connecting the living with the dead. His name was Don Carson. While I would like to elaborate on the specifics of their relationship, my knowledge of Don is limited. He is part of a much greater story that simply isn't mine to tell, but he must be mentioned as he, too, seemed to be present that evening.

As nightfall set in, everyone seated in the ballroom of the inn waited anxiously for Andy to demonstrate how the Probe was operated. Having never seen the actual device up to this point, I had imagined something far more elaborate than what was presented to us that night.

An Inductive Amplifier Tone Probe identical in shape to Andy's with the exception that his was painted black.

Visually, the Probe was nothing spectacular. As I would later learn, it began as a simple electrician's tool called an Inductive Amplifier Tone Probe, which anyone could purchase in a local retail store or online. These devices (unmodified) are used primarily in the telecommunications industry to trace electrical wiring. Andy had modified the internal components (modification specifics were never provided to me), and had painted the device solid black.

Andy sat in the center of the room on a couch holding the Probe. Each person in attendance was asked to shut down the power to their cell phones, and all of the lights in the room were turned off. It wasn't completely dark, however, as ambient light from outside filtered in through the windows of the ballroom. I chose a seat approximately ten feet away, and waited patiently for something to happen.

The room fell silent as Andy switched on the device. Minutes passed before the slight buzzing emanating from the Probe began to grow gradually louder. Andy spoke, and asked if Don were present. A male voice, which wasn't initially clear, answered him. I will admit that I was rather shocked, and cannot remember the exact flow of that conversation. I know

I studied Andy as intently as I could; watching his every move to be sure the group was not being fooled by some hidden trickery. If he was faking it somehow, I could not detect his method.

One by one, individuals asked if they might have a turn at speaking to someone they had loved and previously lost. With each request, Don indicated that he would try to locate them. I must have witnessed half a dozen conversations that night between the people in the room with me and what appeared to be their deceased loved ones. Men, women, children... voices of different ages, with varying accents and inflections were all clearly heard coming from the Probe.

This went on for hours, and I sat there silent, unable to fully wrap my mind around what seemed to be happening right there in front of me. These beautifully touching conversations were reducing adults to tears. As the evening wore on, Andy appeared to grow quite tired and the session with the Probe concluded.

I didn't know how to absorb it. If this were real, and the Probe was doing what it appeared to be doing, it would most certainly change how the world viewed death and our ability to exist beyond it. My mind was racing with questions, and I did not sleep well that night after making it back to my hotel. Time could not have gone by any slower. I knew I had another day and night ahead of me to witness the Probe in action, and it would require rest.

When I arrived at the Black Swan Inn on Saturday, October 9, I knew there would be another session with the Probe that evening. I had come to see the phenomenon for myself, but I had not planned to ask about trying to reach anyone through the device. With every new conversation I witnessed, I grew increasingly anxious. So many questions were running through my mind. Who would I ask to speak to if given the chance? Would they even come through? What sorts of questions would I pose to them? I couldn't keep everything straight in my head. It was extremely overwhelming.

As the late night hours of October 9 turned into the early morning hours of October 10, I waited for an opportunity to ask Andy if I could attempt to reach someone with the Probe. He agreed to let me try. I don't recall the exact hour, but I was already exhausted and sleep deprived. I was worried that if this device was going to fail to work for someone, it was going to be me.

I got up out of my seat from across the room, approached Andy sitting on the couch, and I kneeled down in front of him on the floor. I placed the digital recorder I had brought with me on the coffee table nearby, and was instructed to ask for whomever I wanted to speak to by name. Don, the spirit control, would be asked to help locate them. In that moment, I desperately wanted to hear from my late paternal grandfather Reed.

The next eleven minutes would prove to be one of the most incredibly powerful experiences of my life. The following is a transcript of that conversation, which was recorded not only by me, but by several other

My Grandfather Reed

individuals in attendance. Due to privacy issues, certain sections of that conversation are not detailed here.

As I sat in the dark in the ballroom of the Black Swan Inn that early Sunday morning, Don (the spirit control) was addressed and asked if he could locate my grandfather Reed.

The buzzing from the Probe grew slightly louder, and a voice came through.

DON: "I'll try."

I was told I should call out to my grandfather by name.

APRIL: "Grandpa? Grandpa Reed... Are you there? Will you talk to me please? Me and Jordy really need ya. We really need ya."

Having already witnessed many of these conversations, the weight of actually having the opportunity to try it for myself began to hit me, and I became a little emotional. A voice, faint but obviously male, came through.

REED: "April?"

Andy's research partner Michelle asked who the individual was there to talk to. A moment or two passed without anything being said.

APRIL: "Grandpa, I'm not past begging."

REED: "April??"

The buzzing from the Probe was significantly louder than before when this voice came through› It was *his* voice; my grandfather's. My heart felt like it was going to leap out of my chest when I recognized it. I had not heard this voice in years.

APRIL: "I love you..."

I didn't know what else to say in that moment. I was still reeling from hearing him say my name.

REED: "What's wrong?"

There was obvious concern in his voice, as if some stranger had run up to him with a telephone to tell him he had an emergency phone call on the line. So much was going on in my life at the time, and I momentarily forgot about the numerous other people in the room. What was important to me in that moment was that I seemingly had my grandfather's ear, and there was so much I wanted to talk about.

APRIL: "You died, and something in Jordyn changed. I really need you to help her. Can you help her?"

I tried so hard to remain composed, but I was losing the struggle. Tears were pooling in my eyes as I tried to pull my thoughts together.

REED: "I love you, April."

APRIL: "Do you remember Jordyn? Do you remember the bond you had with her when you were here?"

REED: "I still have that bond."

The tears just kept coming.

REED: "Calm down. Everything's going to be okay. Jordyn will be fine now."

Grandpa had been gone for seven years, but there he was, talking to me. So many memories were running through my mind, but I couldn't help but think of how close he and my children had become while still alive. My grandmother Marilyn (his wife) had passed away just before I had discovered that I was pregnant with my twin daughters, so she never had the opportunity to meet them. Grandpa, however, was with us until the girls were nearly two years old. While he'd already had several great-grandchildren by then, he doted on my daughters, Madison and Jordyn. He had adored them both, but formed a special attachment to Jordyn. The two of them were nearly inseparable. It was as if they were kindred spirits. To know that bond had remained intact despite his death was of great comfort to me.

APRIL: "Am I taking as good a care of her as I'm supposed to be?"

REED: "You're the best."

APRIL: "I don't feel best."

My mind couldn't help but go back to the time when my girls were only five years old. Both were in kindergarten at the time Jordyn experienced the first of what would later turn out to be several seizures. She was quickly diagnosed with epilepsy, and she has continued to struggle with the disorder ever since.

I had often wondered if my grandfather was aware of her condition, and whether or not he thought I was doing all I could as her mother to help her through it. Nobody ever knew it, as I did not discuss it, but from the moment her condition was identified, I felt as though I must somehow be to blame for it. Jordyn's team of doctors could not tell me what was causing the seizures, as all of her scans came back perfectly normal. They were also unable to tell me with any degree of certainty that it wasn't my fault somehow. Maybe I hadn't done something vital while I was pregnant with the twins. There must have been something I did or didn't do, I thought; some sign I missed that would have allowed me to prevent this from happening to my daughter.

I had torn myself up from the inside out for years, agonizing over it every time a seizure occurred. After making sure Jordyn made it through each episode all right, I would hide away in my bedroom closet and completely fall apart. I didn't want anybody to see me; it would only upset them. I suffered on my own, feeling like a complete and utter failure, entirely unfit to be a mother. I'd often sit in that closet, crying, begging God, my late grandparents—anyone that could hear me—to help my little girl. My grandfather must have been there. How else could he have known I blamed myself?

REED: "It's not your fault. Not... your... fault."

In that instant, I lost what little composure I still had left, letting loose a torrent of tears there in front of all of those people. I could hear others in the room crying along with me, as if they too could feel the weight of what had just been said to me. I didn't care anymore if I was being 'professional' or not. This was personal now. I desperately tried to pull myself together before I began speaking again.

APRIL: "I believe it if you say it, Grandpa."

REED: "It's not your fault."

How many times had he witnessed my solitary breakdowns in that closet? His voice was so loving and filled with concern. I took a few moments to let the tears flow, pulled myself together, and continued on with the conversation. I needed to ask him a question that would fully verify the authenticity of the experience for me, beyond what had just occurred.

APRIL: "Can I hear a little bit of the BEE-I-EE song? Can you do that for me?"

One of my most treasured childhood memories is of sitting on my grandfather's knee, listening to the silly songs that he would sing to me. My favorite one was called the BEE-I-EE song, about a little boy who sees and swats at a bee on the wall beside him.

REED: "There was a bee-i-ee, i-ee sat on a wall-i-all, i-all..."

He sang the first line, but much more slowly than he used to, and then stopped to talk to me again.

REED: "Stop crying now."

Everybody in the room laughed, including me. He never did like it when I cried. He had given me the validation I asked for, and he wanted me to be happy about it, not a weeping mess.

APRIL: "Okay, I'll stop. I'll stop. Do you remember the poem I wrote for you?"

REED: "I remember everything you ever did."

This sentiment really touched my heart. It was so simple, but made me realize that when someone dies, they are no longer limited by the constraints of the human brain to access memories. He remembered me, and every moment he and I had spent together.
After I had grown too old to sit on his knee as he sang to me, I wrote him a poem about the memory and how much it had meant to me. He was very proud of it, and often pointed it out to visitors when they came by.

APRIL: "You used to show everybody that poem every time they walked through your front door."

REED: "I'm so proud of you. You're so strong."

I have never considered myself an especially strong person. As hard as I have tried to change it, I wear my heart on my sleeve, and I am often hurt because of it. Before this conversation occurred, I considered it a weakness, but I have since come to realize that it is actually one of my greatest strengths.

APRIL: "I wish I were stronger.... Do you have anything I can tell Dad? He wouldn't believe I could talk to you Grandpa, he wouldn't believe it, but..."

God bless my dad, but my being involved in the paranormal wasn't exactly his wish for me. He often worried (and understandably so) that I was getting into something I shouldn't mess around with. He and I often had conversations where he expressed concern. It was not that he didn't believe in the existence of life after death, he did. I think he has always been afraid that I might stumble into something evil and/or harmful. Most of what I told him I had experienced, he listened to, but didn't fully absorb or believe. How could he trust that I was talking to his late father?

REED: "He won't understand."

I knew he was right. How would I explain any of this to him? It was something I desperately wanted to do, but knew in my heart of hearts that it was not the time.

APRIL: "I know. He misses you a lot and uh, he went up to the house and it's been condemned. Did you know that?"

REED: "Yes."

APRIL: "That hurts my heart."

REED: "It hurts mine, too."

My grandparents' home was located in Ogden, Utah. Much of it, Grandpa had built himself. My dad and his brothers had grown up in that home, and so had I. My grandmother was always so proud of her home, and she had reason to be. It was always so beautifully kept. I was more attached to that house than any "normal" person should have been. After my grandmother died, Grandpa put the house up for sale and moved out. My family had to go through every inch to help pack things up. I couldn't be there to help, as I was living out of state at the time, and I was secretly glad. I could not handle the thought of even one thing being moved out of place. I needed to retain the memory of everything exactly as it was, or I would shatter.

One afternoon, years later, my father called me very upset. He had driven up to the house only to find it in such a neglected state that he just couldn't bear it. He sat on the phone with me and cried. I didn't know how to comfort him, as hearing that people had mistreated something I loved to that degree broke my heart in two.

APRIL: "I love you so much."

REED: "And I love you."

APRIL: "Will you give Grandma a hug for me please?"

REED: "I already did."

I smiled, loving the idea that she was right there with him witnessing this interaction as well.

APRIL: "I love you so much. Do you get the coffee that I leave at the gravestone, and the Werther's, and the toothpicks?"

REED: "Yes. It's okay. This is how it's supposed to be now."

Every time I make the trip back home to Utah, I make it a point to visit the cemetery where my grandparents (and many of my ancestors) are buried, and to bring them both things that they'd loved; a dozen roses for my grandmother, and a cup of coffee with the occasional bag of Werther's Original caramels for my grandfather. I've even left a box of toothpicks a time or two, as Grandpa had a habit of rolling them around between his teeth.

I know that my grandparents are not there in that cemetery, but I have always felt that they not only see these small gestures of remembrance, but that they deeply appreciate them as well. My grandfather confirmed this for me.

APRIL: "Will I get to talk to you again soon?"

REED: "Yes. You *know* you will."

His emphasis on the word "know" reassured me that this would not be my last opportunity to speak to him. How lucky was I to have had *this* conversation? Even if it never happened again, I would still have no right to complain.

APRIL: "I haven't been in the best state of mind lately, and I just needed to know that you're there, so thank you."

REED: "Always."

APRIL: "I love you so much. Go now, and be with Grandma, Robyn, Scotty, and tell them all that I love them, okay?"

REED: "I will. They love you."

Robyn was my aunt, whom I had never met. She died shortly after birth. My uncle Scott had passed recently due to several health complications. I knew they were all together on the other side, and I wanted them to know I was thinking of them.

I began to feel selfish. I knew how much energy it was taking out of me to be a part of the conversation; I couldn't imagine what it was like for my grandfather. I wanted to let him go, but wasn't really ready to do so yet. I still had more questions.

APRIL: "Was that hard to come through this Grandpa? Was it hard?"

REED: "I don't understand it."

He was just as amazed as I was that this was working. I did not expect this to be the case. I suppose there was a large part of me that had always assumed that once a spirit crossed over, they were automatically enlightened with how everything worked on both sides of the veil. I have since discovered that this is not the case. Learning continues, if one wishes to keep learning.

APRIL: "I know, I know. And that's probably because of our religious background, right?"

REED: "It's not supposed to be like this."

APRIL: "I know. I know."

REED: "It's not like we thought."

The entire room took a collective gasp. The weight of this statement hit everyone hard. It was profound for me, in that I had always been religiously taught that things worked in a very specific way once your spirit left your body. Communicating with my grandfather in this way should not have been attempted, or even possible to begin with, according to the religious doctrine I had been taught. Wherever he was, however, it was not as he had expected it to be while living.

I was born and raised in Utah, a member of a family with a rich history in the LDS (or Mormon) faith. My entire extended family were all members of The Church of Jesus Christ of Latter-Day Saints. This was the religion I grew up in, and that was responsible for instilling in me the knowledge that this life was not my beginning, nor would it be my end. I attended church and seminary classes until I married and moved away at the age of twenty. It was, and still remains a huge part of who I am, though I am no longer an active member.

Of all the things I learned in my faith, there was one lesson I am reminded of nearly every day. I was taught that whenever I encountered doubt, I should pray to God with a sincere heart about what was troubling me, and He would make the answer known to me. As I got older, and my list of questions grew, I did exactly as I was taught; only, the answers I received were not at all like the answers my fellow church members bore testimony to having received in their own lives. This distressed me a great deal, as I did not want to disappoint my family with my doubts.

What I loved about the church was its focus on the idea of families being bound together for eternity. It was how this was made possible that the church and I didn't exactly see eye to eye on. Due to this issue (among several others too numerous and complicated to discuss here) I decided it was best for me to keep searching for the answers I was seeking on my own. I wanted to know how the afterlife truly worked, not from reading scripture or listening to lectures, but from connecting with someone who was already *there*. I wanted to share this experience, and everything I was learning from it with my family.

APRIL: "See? And if I could just get that through to Mom and Dad, I think they would be a lot happier."

REED: "Someday, they will."

APRIL: "Will I be a part of helping them understand?"

REED: "Yes."

APRIL: "Okay."

APRIL: "Will you stay with me, please?"

REED: "I never left."

In that instant, I knew Heaven was not a far-off place. He was there, and still able to reach me.

APRIL: "I was the only one who wasn't there when you passed, and I've always felt guilty for that."

REED: "Stop it."

He didn't harbor any resentment toward me for not being there. I needed to hear that. These seemingly little messages had a tremendous impact on me. It was unnecessary for me to hold onto guilt or grief.

APRIL: "Did you pick a fight with Courtney so that you could pass by yourself?"

REED: "What do *you* think?"

94

Grandpa had moved into my parent's home so they could better care for him in his old age, even though they both continued to work full-time jobs. My sister Courtney often stayed with him while she studied for school. As his condition deteriorated, his temper would flare over simple things, and he became difficult to get along with. Living in Washington State at the time, I was never witness to this, but I knew how hard it was on my family back home.

One afternoon, Grandpa had become a little belligerent with Courtney over a misunderstanding with a shopping errand. It seemed a strange thing to argue about, and his attitude had deeply hurt her feelings. She told him that if he was going to yell at her, he'd have to take care of himself from then on, and she left the house in tears. Grandpa was left to assume that Courtney would not be back the next day, but of course, she did return to help take care of him.

Both of my parents had already left for work when Courtney arrived just after 8:00 a.m. the next morning.

"When I walked into his bedroom, it felt like there were a hundred other people in the room. I don't know how else to describe the atmosphere of it," she told me. "I looked at Grandpa lying on his side in bed and I knew… I just knew he was gone."

My grandfather passed away peacefully in his sleep. In discussing that morning's events with my sister, I knew she felt a huge sense of guilt for not having been there with him in his final moments.

"But he wasn't alone, Courtney. You said so yourself," I said. "You felt all of the people who loved him and passed before him right there in that room."

She listened to me, but I don't think she ever really believed that as much as I did. I believed then, as I do now, that it is often difficult for the people we love to let go and move on if we are always nearby. Even if it doesn't seem that they are cognizant of our sorrow, they are, and I can't imagine it is easy for them to leave us in such a state. I believe my grandfather knew his time was nearing, and he wanted to be alone when that time came. Of course, I don't think it was his intention to hurt Courtney's feelings; I just feel he was frustrated and ready to go.

APRIL: "I know you. I will tell her that it's not her fault. Is that okay?"

95

REED: "It was nobody's fault."

APRIL: "I know it's not like we thought. I've always known that and..."

REED: "It's beautiful."

APRIL: (crying) "I know it's beautiful... because you're there."

He was in a beautiful place, and I was happy to hear it. As I look back on my conversation with him, I wish I would have delved deeper into the details, but I knew I was running out of time with him. His voice, along with the buzzing that accompanied it on the Probe, was weakening.

APRIL: "I'm a good person, right Grandpa?"

REED: "You're the best."

APRIL: "I'm on the path I'm supposed to be on, right?"

REED: "Yes."

APRIL: "I just love you so much, and just wish I could hug you, Grandpa, I do."

REED: "Do it."

APRIL: "I will do it. I will."

REED: "I'm here for you."

APRIL: "Protect my babies, okay?"

REED: "I already do. I've gotta go, Sugar."

APRIL: "That's okay. Go ahead and go. Thank you so much. I love you. I'll talk to you soon. G'night, Grandpa."

And with that, the Probe slowly fell silent. I stood up, turned off my recorder, and walked outside. On the front step of the Inn, staring up at the stars, the world around me looked entirely different. It was a little difficult for me to catch my breath. Everything seemed so surreal, as if what had just happened to me had all been a dream.

In the span of eleven minutes, much of my despair and hopelessness had been lifted from me. Aside from the birth of my children, it was the single most amazing gift I had ever been given. I thought to myself, *This is it. Every answer I've been searching for, I've found.* There was a sense of finality I felt that night that lead me to believe I had no further reason to continue on with the research. How could anything I experience from that point on even compare? I didn't have a Probe of my own to work with, and I certainly couldn't go back to the way I'd always done things before.

Sharing the Experience

I felt anxious to share what had just happened with members of my immediate family. By that time, it was nearly four o'clock in the morning. The only person I could risk waking with a phone call was my sister Courtney. After several rings, she answered.

"Hello? April, is something wrong?" she asked sleepily.

"You're not going to believe me," I said, "But I just talked to Grandpa."

"What? What are you talking about? Is this a joke?"

I fumbled with my words, desperately trying to make sense of what had just happened in my own head while trying to articulate the details to my sister. I told her that the entire conversation had been recorded, and I'd be happy to let her hear it as soon as I made it back to Dallas. She was patient and kind despite my having roused her in the middle of the night, but I could tell she didn't quite believe what I was trying to tell her. I felt relieved that I had at least been able to tell one member of my family about what had happened.

In the days and weeks that followed, I found that sharing the details of the event with anyone, especially members of my own family, would prove difficult if not altogether impossible. This event had happened to me, and more importantly, *for* me. I'd barely had time to ingest the information I'd been given, and to accept its method of delivery as a reality. Talking to the dead was normal to me, and yet this experience had shaken me. How could I expect others to readily accept it?

Shortly after returning home from the event at the Black Swan Inn, I began writing about the experience and sharing the information online in various blogs and posts. The reactions were unsurprisingly mixed, but people were paying attention, and questions began pouring in from every direction. In a matter of months, I was being asked to speak at different paranormal events to share my story. To be honest, I was terrified of accepting such invitations as I have always been more comfortable flying under the radar, but I did accept, and found myself speaking to large audiences about the night my grandfather came to talk to me.

At the end of every presentation, people approached me in tears to tell me they had been deeply touched by the story and that they appreciated my willingness to share something so personal. While it was never my intention to make people cry, it was nice to know that the message I was trying to convey was reaching them in a meaningful way.

The more I became a public figure, the more my family and friends wanted to know about the work I was doing, so they asked me to present the same information to them that I had been presenting at conferences. This intimidated me. Standing in front of a room full of strangers and pouring your heart out is difficult, but doing it for those you know and love (who also hold onto a great many misconceptions about what it is you do) is infinitely harder.

My father had not heard the audio recording of the ITC conversation I'd had with Grandpa. We talked about it from time to time, but he struggled with the idea that such a conversation was even possible. He and my mother were both front and center the day I spoke and played a majority of the recording for those who came to hear it. When the presentation was concluded, audience members asked me questions but also posed questions to my parents about their thoughts on it.

"I don't know if that was really my father's voice or not," my dad replied. "But it doesn't really matter what I believe. If April believes it's him, and it has helped her through whatever difficulties she's faced, then I support her."

Hearing my father say that was a gift in and of itself. Knowing my mother held the same opinion helped ease a great deal of worry that I constantly carried with me. I did not want to be a disappointment to them for pursuing the research I loved. It healed my heart a great deal to know that I hadn't. They might not have always understood it, or even agreed with it, but they accepted it. They accepted me, and that meant everything.

-8-
Unexpected Consequences

"Do not forget the dead, unless they are strong enough to be happy without your remembrance; but do not lean too heavily upon them... the ordinary soul is very sensitive to the call of those it loved on earth."
X, Letters From the Afterlife

The euphoria I felt after speaking with my grandfather lasted for days afterward. I believe I went into a state of shock, as I couldn't sleep, eat, or concentrate on anything else. It was a beautiful feeling. I wanted to share it with everyone I knew, but I didn't know how to do that without making them all think I was crazy. Too many people in my life already viewed me as "odd." Telling them I had spoken to my late grandfather among a room full of strangers would seem more than just a little irrational.

After arriving home and finally getting a bit of rest, I thought everything was back to normal. Life was different, of course. I felt so grateful for the gift I had been given, and found that I was able to handle certain stresses a lot easier than before. But, as the days wore on, I began to feel deeply saddened.

When someone close to us passes away, we grieve. We go through the motions of letting go and saying goodbye, feeling an immense sorrow for their loss. We try to resolve ourselves to the thought that for as long as we live, we'll not have the opportunity again to wrap our arms around that person or to have their arms wrapped around us. At the time I had the ITC conversation with my grandfather, he had been deceased for seven years. I had already been through the process of burying him once. I had not expected to feel as though I were doing that all over again.

To hear the voice of someone I'd loved and lost, years after their passing, was both miraculous and devastating in its effect. For a brief period of time, I had my grandfather there in the room with me again, telling me that he loved me and was deeply proud of the person I'd become. But, when that time with him ended, I grieved his loss a second time. This was an unexpected consequence of the connection, and one I caution everyone to consider when attempting spirit communication to this degree. There are reasons why it is often difficult to reach our dead. When we do, our lives and everything we believe to be true can be turned entirely upside down.

As thrilling as it may seem to speak to the dead, I doubt many consider how life-altering it can truly be. After all, most of those involved in paranormal investigation aren't hearing from their deceased relatives on their EVP recordings, or having long conversations with them via ITC devices. Investigations are largely conducted in the homes and businesses of others, where the interaction between the living and the dead is buffered with unfamiliarity. How many spirits had reached out to me in the years before the ITC conversation with my grandfather? I couldn't even venture a guess, but they had all been strangers to me. I had never known them while they were alive. I was able to interact with them, absorb the experience for what it was, and then put it down and move on. It's a much more difficult task to disconnect when the person on the other end of the line is someone you love.

There has not been a day since that ITC conversation occurred that I have not thought of how much I miss my grandfather, and how wonderful it would be to talk to him again. He had said that we'd have the opportunity to talk again, but I wasn't given any details as to how that would be made possible.

An Inductive Amplifier of My Own

In the months following the ITC event at the Black Swan Inn, Andy Coppock and I kept in touch, and we often discussed his work with the amplifier. Naturally, I wanted a similar device of my own to work with, but I knew he was being bombarded with requests from the paranormal community. I'd already had a profound experience with it, and felt that requesting a device would be a selfish thing to do. And so, I did not ask.

During a trip out to Texas in January of 2011, Andy and his partner Michelle made a visit to my home. They delivered a clearer digital recording of my ITC conversation with my grandfather, which pleased me a great deal. They stayed for dinner, and as the evening wore on, Andy said he had something to tell me. I was to be given an amplifier to use for my own

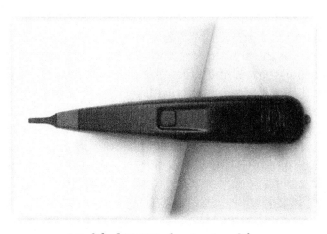
Modified EMF Inductive Amplifier

research! Naturally, I was elated at the news, albeit a bit shocked. When I asked why I had been chosen to receive one, his answer was that I was someone who "got it" and would use the technology in the correct way and with the best of intentions. While sitting on my living room couch discussing the particulars, he received a text message on his cell phone.

"You're not going to believe this," Andy said, "But I just got a text message from individuals at a lab in New Mexico who have been observing an amplifier and reporting back to me whenever it 'says' anything. This particular Probe hasn't been active at all lately, but tonight it apparently said, 'April Slaughter.'"

He was correct; I found that difficult to believe, but a part of me *wanted* to believe it. I took him at his word, and thought that if it were true, perhaps those on the other side of the veil wanted me to have an amplifier because they knew, just as Andy did, that I would not abuse the privilege.

The following month, during a trip to Southern California to visit my sister, Andy drove down to San Diego and hand-delivered an inductive amplifier. He had made all the necessary modifications. The external housing of the device was slightly different than the amplifier he himself worked with, but I was assured it had all of the right components in place to operate correctly.

All I was instructed to do was to keep the amplifier close, spend time working with it when I could, and be patient for the results that Andy was sure would come. Having worked for years with the various radio devices, I knew that it would take time to establish a connection, if and when one was meant to be established. Yet, I desperately wanted it to work the first time I turned it on. After Andy left, I sat on my sister's couch for several hours, running the amplifier. Nothing happened, but I was not discouraged.

The Amplifier Comes to Life

I returned to Texas eager to begin working with the amplifier. As I had with Frank's Box and the MiniBox, I began setting time aside in the evenings to experiment in the comfort of my own home. I kept meticulous notes about current weather conditions, my emotional state, how long the amplifier had been run, what questions had been asked, and details of any strange happenings that either manifested directly from the amplifier or in the surrounding environment while it was functioning. I didn't want to miss anything. I recorded every session on my digital recorder for later review, as well. Months passed, with the same routine being repeated over and over again. Every once in awhile, a strange knocking sound would be heard in the house, or a fluctuation in the intensity of the white noise from the device would be significant enough for me to take notice, but there were no voices.

When the amplifier failed to produce anything of note at home, I decided to try working with it at a "haunted" location. Up until this point, my team members with The Paranormal Source, Inc. had only heard about the amplifier, and had not yet been given the opportunity to witness it in action.

As a group, we arranged an investigation of the now-closed and privately owned Yorktown Memorial Hospital in Yorktown, Texas. The property was familiar to me, as I had investigated it several times before. It is one of the more consistently active locations for paranormal phenomena

Yorktown Memorial Hospital – Yorktown, Texas

that I have ever visited, and I thought it would be the perfect place to test the amplifier. After all, it was in this very hospital that Andy Coppock had recorded the first amplifier ITC conversation I'd initially heard, and the one that convinced me to attend the event at the Black Swan Inn. If the spirits residing in the hospital were willing to talk to him, perhaps they would be willing to talk to me.

As we wandered around the hospital, the groundskeeper, Mike Henson, accompanied us and described several recent incidents that had occurred on the property. Apparitions, screams heard from deep inside the building in the middle of the night, objects moving on their own... all of these things were fairly commonplace at Yorktown.

We spent hours broken up into different groups, wandering the hallways, snapping photographs, recording audio, and doing all of the typical things investigative groups do. A few of my team members reported that they'd seen odd shadow movements, heard whispery conversations, and experienced extreme changes in temperature. As the evening wore on, we decided to regroup and spend some time in the basement. We pulled a circle of chairs together in the area where the four hallways in the basement intersect.

I switched on the amplifier, and asked for a few different individuals by name that we had connected with in the past to come and try to speak with us through the device. A slight buzzing was consistent and normal, but when Mike joined the group and sat down next to me, the buzzing gradually became louder. At nearly the same moment, several members of the team began seeing a shadow move toward the end of one of the hallways. One of the investigators got up to try and identify what the source of the shadow might be. Once he reached the end, several of us watched as what appeared to be another person walk from one side of the hallway to the other, between our group and the investigator at the end of the hall. Something was definitely happening.

While I held the amplifier in my lap, another investigator began snapping photographs down the hallway. His first attempt failed, as the flash did not fire correctly, but he managed to correct the issue and he took several more photographs. Suddenly, the sound from the amplifier grew so loud that the buzzing was almost unbearable to listen to. Whatever was affecting it seemed to be growing in strength. Seemingly out of nowhere, and with no reasonable explanation, Mike began to feel ill and said he needed to step outside for a little fresh air. As soon as he got up to leave, the signal from the amplifier quieted, and further attempts to reestablish a connection failed. The remainder of the evening was quite calm and uneventful, but I felt as though I had made some progression with the device.

When my team began reviewing their data, several of them sent me audio clips in which a female voice was clearly heard speaking through the static. The voice did not belong to any of those in attendance that night. The investigator whose camera flash seemed to temporarily malfunction sent me a photograph he'd nearly deleted before he noticed something odd about it. When I received the image, it took me a moment to identify the anomaly, but when I did, I was taken aback. In order for the image to be seen in print, it had to be inverted to allow the figure to be clearly identified. I sent the original image file to a professional photographer to examine, and it was his opinion that the image had not been altered in any way. The figure in the photograph had not been digitally manufactured.

A woman, dressed in a long gown cinched at the waist, with her hand on her hip is almost instantly identifiable. The apparition was not seen with the naked eye at the time the photograph was taken, so her head and face were unknowingly excluded, but it is still a compelling image. "She" could not have been more than a few feet away from the group.

Whoever she was, I believe she had put in a great deal of effort to connect with us that evening, and the closer she came to the amplifier, the louder it grew. When the session was interrupted, the activity dissipated, and we were unable to experience it again.

After the incident at Yorktown, I returned home with a renewed enthusiasm about the inductive amplifier. I was not looking to connect with the spirits of random individuals; I wanted to hear from my grandfather.

For weeks, I followed the usual routine when running the amp with little to no success. One evening, after I grew particularly tired and irritated, I held the device in my hand and said, "Grandpa? Can you hear me? Are you even there? You told me you'd come talk to me again, but I haven't heard from you. I think I might be close to giving up."

"HERE!"

The loud and immediate response startled me.

"Grandpa?" I asked again.

Nothing.

The amplifier once again went silent. I left it on for another hour or so hoping that the voice would speak again, but it did not. Little by little, the hope that I'd once again converse with anyone using the amplifier began slipping away from me.

-9-
The Shadow of Doubt

"If you would be a real seeker after truth, it is necessary that at least once in your life you doubt, as far as possible, all things."
René Descartes

As days turned into weeks and weeks turned into months, I began feeling as though there would be no amount of time I could invest with the amplifier to make it work as well as it had when I'd first experienced it. The occasional word or two would be clearly heard, but a conversation with one or more individuals was not happening for me. I was spending my nights sleepless, waiting for a familiar voice to pierce the silence and once again inspire me to keep moving forward with the work I loved to do, but that voice never came, and an all-consuming doubt began etching away at my faith.

It was not simply the lack of response from the other side that contributed to my doubts, as time and persistence would have been enough to rectify that. Life had set out to challenge me in many ways; not just with my research, but with almost every aspect of my life.

Jordyn's seizures had worsened significantly. Every doctor, every medication, every holistic attempt at healing was failing, and therefore I felt once again that I as her mother was failing her as well. One afternoon, she was walking across the living room toward the kitchen when she suddenly fell to the floor, flailing uncontrollably like I had never before witnessed. Madison (her twin sister) began to cry as I asked her to bring me the phone so that I could call 911. I held Jordyn in my arms, looked into her eyes, and she just wasn't there. Her breathing stopped, and her lips turned blue. With my little girl still convulsing in my arms, I screamed at the dispatcher to hurry and send an ambulance.

"You can't leave me, baby girl," I cried. "Come back. Breathe... please breathe!"

Moments later, the rigidity of her body faded, her eyes blinked, and she took a long deep breath. As the color returned to her face she said, "I heard you, Mom. I went away for a while, but I came back. I'll always come back."

EMTs ran through the front door seconds after she recovered from the seizure. They took her vitals, and then the three of us were loaded up into the ambulance. As she often does after an episode, Jordyn had fallen asleep, and remained unconscious all the way to the hospital where a series of tests awaited her. It was not our first such experience, but Jordyn's seizures had mostly been what are often referred to as "staring spells" and not the grand mal type (or tonic clonic as they are called today.) I was terrified and exhausted. After blood tests, a CT scan, and several hours waiting in the emergency room, Jordyn was discharged, and I had no answers. All the test results came back normal, and I was left to wonder if this would be an isolated incident. It was not.

My daughters' school was less than a mile from our house, but every time its number showed up on caller ID when my phone rang, my heart leapt into my throat. It became a race between me and the ambulance to make it to the school first. I usually won. Jordyn suffered several severe seizures during her fourth grade year that I knew had nearly taken her from me, and no one had any answers. It was just a matter of time before the next seizure hit, and I had no way of predicting when it would come, or how it would end.

Finding Flaws in the Recollection

Calm down. Everything's going to be okay. Jordyn will be fine now...

That's what my grandfather had said that night in 2010. Fine now? Things were not fine; they'd only gotten worse.

The ITC conversation as printed in this book is not complete. The discussion I'd had with the spirit of my grandfather with regard to Jordyn's affliction was a bit more detailed and personal than what I was able to include. To paraphrase the missing pieces, there were certain individuals discussed that my grandfather asked me to trust in helping my daughter win her battle with epilepsy. One of these individuals in particular had entered my life and had offered me a possible new solution to believe in. This person won my trust, came into my home, spent time with my children, and strung me along with an elaborate lie. There was never any intention of helping her. When I realized my daughter and I had been conned, my entire world caved in. I would eventually learn that I was not the first individual to have been deceived in such a way, nor was I the last. This person inflicted the one wound I am likely never to recover from, and one I will certainly never forgive.

If my grandfather's spirit had truly come to talk to and comfort me, he would not have asked me to trust someone capable of inflicting so much damage. He would never have knowingly sent me down a path he could see would only end in devastation. No, I did not expect my grandfather (or anyone else on the other side) to be somehow all-knowing, but if he'd been wrong about asking me to trust this person, he'd have found a way to warn me, and no such warning came.

Will I get to talk to you again soon?
Yes. You know you will.

As of the date of publication, I have not heard from my grandfather again via Instrumental Transcommunication using any of the devices I have at my disposal. If the communication in 2010 had been genuine (and facilitated by a stranger) why had he not returned to speak directly to me, someone he loved and had always been connected to? I did everything I had been instructed to do; followed every unwritten rule. Certainly, he was aware of my daughter's suffering, as well as my own.

Will you stay with me please?
I never left.

I was dealing with my daughter's epilepsy largely on my own. All of my family and friends lived out of state. If my grandfather was still with me, I was unable to detect him. I had never felt so entirely alone in all of my life.

Community Backlash

Anyone who has attempted to create a device or method to enable direct communication between the living and the dead has certainly been no stranger to skepticism and harsh criticism. It is par for the course. When the inductive amplifier was introduced to the paranormal community, many threw themselves behind it while others stopped at nothing to discredit the device and those publicly using it. Normally such things do not sway my personal opinion, but I found I was unable to ignore what the critics were saying.

I am no scientist, but there are many in the research field who are. The questions they were posing to the various developers of ITC devices were legitimate, but most of them went unanswered. The controversy evolved into a game of who could do the most damage to the other's reputation, and it was obvious to me that it was mainly just for sport. Still, something in the back of my mind kept nagging at me. I knew from personal experience that the amplifier worked. Beyond my initial experience, the amp had produced interesting results when I had operated it entirely on my own. However, I had worked tirelessly with the amp for over two years, and had not been able to carry on a continual conversation with my grandfather or any other spirit.

On one hand, I could validate the eleven-minute ITC session in many ways, and yet, on the other, many aspects of it became increasingly more suspicious. I grew angry at the fact that I had spent a great deal of time and energy publicly supporting people and instruments whose potential had been given far more credit than they might have deserved. I had agreed to speak at public functions because I believed in the work I thought was being done, and its ability to further understanding about the afterlife.

As I look back on it all now, I have come to view the situation in a particular way. Before ITC had become part of my research, I had already come to the conclusion that ghosts/spirits existed and interacted with the living more so than most people would like to think about or accept. It was and has remained an unmovable foundation, solid and strong. The accumulated experiences I've piled on top of that foundation have not always been without fault, but while some have become weakened and fallen away, my resolve to rebuild remains. If at any point I have been deliberately deceived, that rests on the shoulders of those who have reveled in the deception, and I wholeheartedly believe there will come a time when they will be forced to answer for it.

When One Door Closes...

Though my will to continue on as a public figure in the paranormal community was undoubtedly wavering, I knew in my heart that I would never be able to fully separate myself from the work. So much of who I am and how I live my life is a direct result of all that I have personally experienced with the supernatural, and there is no walking away from that. I needed direction if I was going to keep making some sort of difference; if in fact I'd ever really made a difference at all.

I had learned the hard way that it was important for me to keep my eyes and ears open, listen to many, but trust very few. I let go of all of my expectations, asked for a sign as to what it was I needed to do, and just continued living. It was the best I could do. When next I approached an "open door" that showed signs of promise and progression, I prayed I'd have the courage to walk through it.

-10-
Induced After-Death Communication

"The dead make the best therapists."
Allan L. Botkin, Ph.D.

Life had unraveled for me in 2011. Almost everyone who spent time with me began noticing that I was not at all my usual self. I drew inward, while pushing those around me away. I didn't know how else to deal with the overwhelming disappointments I had suffered. I felt – and acted – completely lost. In all honesty, I wanted nothing more to do with paranormal research or most of the individuals involved in it. To think about it brought me a great deal of pain, and I felt I had already done my fair share of suffering.

I stopped working with the various ITC devices, including the inductive amplifier. They had fallen largely silent for months, and I began to feel as though both the living and the dead had abandoned me. I hardly noticed that I had been neglecting my investigation team members and friends. All I wanted to do was pour all of my energy into taking care of my children. After all, they were my only constant source of comfort and love. They had always been my main priority, but now they were the only real peace I knew. My marriage suffered (and would eventually end) as did my writing. The purpose in life I thought I'd found, I'd lost, and I became a shell of the person I once was.

One morning, while mindlessly playing around online, I thought I'd take a look at what books had recently been released. I logged into my Amazon account, and a list of suggestions was waiting for me. One book in particular caught my eye: *Induced After-Death Communication: A New Therapy*

For Healing Grief and Trauma by Dr. Allan L. Botkin. I briefly read its description, and while it sounded interesting, my heart just wasn't into delving back into a subject that I had been trying to avoid. Over the next several weeks, the book kept showing up in different places online, and I found it increasingly difficult to ignore. I eventually caved, and purchased a copy. When it arrived, I put it on my office bookshelf, where it sat collecting dust. I turned my attention to other things, knowing that if and when I ever began to feel like reading about paranormal topics again, it would be there.

I can't say what inspired me to finally pick up the book and read it, but once I did, I couldn't put it down. It was not at all what I had expected it to be. For several hours, I sat and devoured one chapter after another until I had read the book in its entirety.

All of my life, I had been searching for ways to connect to and communicate with the spirits of those who had passed on, and I had achieved that in a variety of ways. I had worked with some of the most well-known names in the paranormal research field, and I desperately wanted the work I had attempted to do to make a positive difference in the lives of others. Due to the devastation I had recently endured, I began to feel as though I had nothing left to contribute, nothing new to experience that could reignite my desire to keep looking for answers.

By the time I had finished Dr. Botkin's book, I felt as though the universe (or perhaps even the spirits of those I loved) had repeatedly brought it to my attention for a reason, and that it was no coincidence that I was being introduced to IADC at this particular point in time. Instrumental Transcommunication (ITC) had provided me with answers and experiences beyond anything I had previously imagined, but IADC was an entirely different approach, one that I had never known anyone in the paranormal field to research or discuss.

What is IADC?

Induced After-Death Communication (IADC) is a controversial technique used in psychotherapy to help patients face, process, and recover from severe grief and trauma. Those who have undergone the procedure report seeing and conversing with the spirits of their deceased loved ones, resulting in a drastic reduction or complete elimination of their associated grief. This technique was discovered and perfected by Dr. Botkin during his many years of work with Vietnam veterans in Chicago. In the years since its initial successes he has trained numerous psychotherapists around the world to perform the IADC procedure for their patients.

Typically, three sessions are scheduled. During the first session, grief that the patient is experiencing is discussed before Eye Movement Desensitization and Reprocessing (EMDR) is administered. EMDR is a technique which does not rely on a dialogue between the therapist and the patient. Instead, it uses the patient's own rapid eye movement to trigger emotional processing in the brain. It has been shown to quickly and effectively uncover the "core sadness" the individual is grappling with, briefly accelerating the emotion, and then decreasing it dramatically.

The second session is when the IADC experience usually occurs. EMDR, in a particular sequence, is administered again. This assists the patient in connecting with what they believe to be the spirit of the individual(s) they are grieving. Patients often report seeing, hearing, and even touching those they'd lost, helping them to resolve any unfinished business and to move past their grief. These experiences typically last anywhere from a few seconds to several minutes, and cannot be predicted or controlled by either the therapist or the patient.

During the third session, the patient returns to the therapist to discuss the experience and to address any issues still outstanding. If need be, the experience can be induced again to resolve any remaining grief associated with the deceased.

The IADC experience is unique to every individual who undergoes the procedure. The patient is (except in rare cases) the only individual to perceive the event. Trained therapists agree that while it seems to help their patients process their grief, they cannot claim that they are actually speaking to the dead.

The religious and/or spiritual beliefs of patients do not seem to guide or affect the experience in any way. The results are the same in that patients are reconnected to and healed by those who have loved them and passed on, regardless of whether or not the patient believes in an afterlife.

There has never been—among the thousands of documented cases—an instance where the patient reported encountering anything negative in nature during their IADC, even if they had some pre-conceived notion that they might. In fact, most (if not all) patients leave their therapist's office following their IADC experience with a complete and lasting resolution of their grief.

An Afternoon with Dr. Botkin

Upon finishing the book, I was certain of two things: one, that I wanted to sit down with Dr. Botkin to discuss the IADC phenomenon, and two, that I wanted nothing more than to experience it firsthand. As it turned out, I would have the opportunity to do both.

I contacted Dr. Botkin, who graciously agreed to meet with me while I was traveling through Illinois in the spring of 2012. I was armed with a list of questions, but wasn't sure how well they would be received. I knew from what he had written that he was not claiming that IADCs were proof of the existence of an

Dr. Allan L. Botkin, Psy.D.

afterlife, but putting that aside, I wanted to know how he personally felt about it. Dr. Botkin's profession and mine are worlds apart, but I felt as though we had a common goal of taking some of the fear and sorrow that accompanies death and replacing it with a little hope and healing by encouraging a sustained connection to those we love.

"I've spent years communicating with the dead using various technical devices," I began. "But you've discovered a way for the human brain to be open to doing the same thing on its own, using EMDR. Why do you suppose it works so well?"

"I'm not sure," said Dr. Botkin. "Many people who use standard EMDR therapy have the desire to come and have me train them because while they've been administering the eye movements, their patients have often had spontaneous after-death communications, so it wasn't just my observation. There's something about the bilateral stimulation that enables that. It puts the brain into a much higher processing mode. I use it to get people to a peaceful state of mind. Once their sadness starts to fall away, my patients often tell me that the calm and peacefulness they experience feels good to them. It is in that calm state that they are open and ready for the ADC. I always tend to think of it as being on a level of higher vibration. Sometimes I think the people on the other side see us in slow motion. When we're sad, we're like molasses. The bilateral stimulation increases the brain's processing so things speed up. This helps reduce the sadness, and when you do the induction you speed the brain up again so it's in that higher mode. I think we have to reach a higher frequency level so that we better match theirs."

I was fascinated to hear this, because in my own personal experiences with spirit communication, I had been told on more than one occasion that those on the other side often see us as slow and fuzzy shapes. I didn't quite grasp the reason why but it was beginning to make a lot more sense to me now that Dr. Botkin was able to share his view on vibration with me.

"While a patient is experiencing an IADC, have you ever asked them to inquire about something with the deceased on your behalf?"

"Yes," he said. "In fact, there's an instance in the book that was my favorite. I was working with a former Marine sergeant in Chicago, a real just-the-facts type of guy. He was not the type to embellish anything, just a real straight shooter. He had some of the most beautiful ADCs. At one point, he was talking to a man he'd known in his past, and the deceased was telling him all of these things about the other side that he wasn't even asking about. I asked my patient if he would be willing to ask a question for me. He said he would try, so I asked, 'Is inducing ADCs a good thing?' The spirit of this man replied, saying yes it was, and that humans needed to know about the spirit world. He also said, 'Do not fool yourself. We are always in control of the experience... not you.' And that made absolute perfect sense to me.

"My only role in the procedure is to help clear the immense sadness, all of that slow-motion painful kind of stuff. EMDR revs up the brain of the patient and then at that point I step back and the deceased completely control the experience. When the patient tries to control what is happening, the ADC stops. It has to unfold naturally."

"Surely the dead are aware of what you are doing to help people," I said. "Have your patients ever relayed such a message to you from individuals they connect with during their ADCs?"

"Yes. It actually gives me goose bumps. A deceased individual in one of my patient's ADCs said that when I die, not only will my friends and family be there to greet me, but all of the spirits who were connected with the living in ADCs to thank me. It's an overwhelming thought. It would be like a stadium full of people!"

"I read your book and thought that the dead have to be thankful to you for doing what you do," I said.

"I get a number of messages saying that I should keep working with people in this way, and not to stop. Once, while working with a woman who was about twenty-two, she connected with the spirit of her late brother who had drowned in a swimming pool. She had described seeing a pinpoint of light as the ADC began, and it grew increasingly larger as it drew closer. This is how her brother began to appear to her. She was one of the most spiritually gifted people I'd ever worked with and her experiences were really amazing.

"Between the sessions I'd had with her, I woke up one morning at 4 a.m. As I laid there with my eyes closed, I distinctly saw a small pinpoint of light, which I thought was rather odd as I still hadn't opened my eyes. I figured it would most likely disappear once I opened them, but as I did, the light was still there, and it moved across the ceiling. When next I sat with this young woman, I told her about my experience, and in another ADC, she was able to ask her brother if he had been responsible for the light I'd seen. He said, 'Yes it was me! I did it to encourage you to continue doing the work you're doing.'"

To know the dead were aware of Dr. Botkin's work and that they appreciated it was encouraging to me. I had been told on many occasions (even during the eleven-minute ITC conversation with my grandfather) that the work I was doing was worthwhile. It meant something, and positive things could come from it. While the method of delivery was quite different, the message to Dr. Botkin was the same. Of course, his work was far more profound than anything I had done. He was helping to heal people.

"I assume there are people in your field of psychotherapy who don't really believe in any of this," I said.

"Yes, there are. I remember one instance in particular that was upsetting to me. After Whitney Houston's passing, her daughter appeared on the *Oprah Winfrey Show* and was talking about how she had seen her mother's spirit. Dr. Drew was also on the show, and referred to her experience as nothing more than a 'grief hallucination.' I remember getting so mad listening to that. He predicted that this girl would take a turn for the worse once the 'hallucinations' stopped and would most likely suffer alone in pain. My prediction is the opposite."

In all of the cases Dr. Botkin outlined in his book, there had not been any patients whose overwhelming grief returned, even after a significant length of time had passed since their IADC experiences. In his book, he states:

"If the IADC phenomenon is hallucination, it is a grander hallucination than any ever recorded in the annals of psychology."

"It convinces the patient, counter to the person's embedded, intransigent, negative emotions, that a deceased person feels differently than the patient believed, and the directions of that different feeling is always positive, in spite of the fact that the patient's traumatic images have all been intensely negative, at times for decades. The healing savant faculty supersedes the person's normal perceptual framework, diagnoses the person's needs, views life and the traumatic events from another perspective, reorients perceptions without influence from the therapist or the person's own consciousness, and sends the mind on its way, blissfully, miraculously, and irreversibly healed."

"Instead of encouraging acceptance of the feelings of disconnection and withdrawal from emotional attachment to the deceased, IADC therapy actually provides psychological resolution through the profound, life-changing experience of reconnection with the deceased. Their sense of love and unbroken connection is renewed by an uplifting experience that gives them the feeling of a different but satisfying and permanent new relationship with the deceased. They rebuild meaning through the new relationship, and they continue their bond knowing their loved one is OK and imminent. The experience of reconnection heals."

"It has no residual negative side effects. Patients aren't prone to other hallucinations; they don't lose touch with reality; and they aren't more likely to be hospitalized for pathologies associated with hallucinations."

His success rate with being able to induce these experiences with his patients was impressive, but I had read in the book that it didn't always work with every attempt or with every individual.

"About seventy-six percent of my patients have successful IADCs. Roughly a quarter do not. In those cases, however, there's usually something psychological getting in the way. Some people have too much internal chatter going on all the time, and have no sense of how to shut that off. Some just can't. They'll sit there with their eyes closed and think to themselves, '*Gee, I sure hope this works. I hope I don't screw it up somehow,*' and that keeps the experience from happening."

I told Dr. Botkin that I felt too much internal chatter was also an issue with those in the paranormal community who desperately wanted to experience something supernatural, but always seemed unable to. There is this pre-conceived idea that we experience the presence of spirits only in a limited number of ways. Those who are largely skeptical about the existence of ghosts (and our ability to interact with them) cannot be satisfied by subtle signs. Short of an apparition taking shape and shaking hands with them, some people will never believe.

"You know, I personally never understood the ghost-hunting thing," he said. "Spirits being mischievous and such. I've never encountered a dead person that was trying to scare me or cause me any trouble."

"Many are wrapped up in the idea that ghosts are frightening, that their presence signifies something negative or demonic. That hasn't been my experience at all," I replied.

Dr. Botkin and I discussed the popular opinion among believers that those who die sudden or tragic deaths are somehow stuck wandering on this plane of existence.

"I've worked with a lot of people," he began. "Many of whom had died suddenly, and they weren't lost at all. Take those who lost their lives in Vietnam, for example. Those who've come through in ADCs never talk of being unhappy or in the wrong place. I believe a lot of mythology has been passed down over time. These new discoveries are helping us to sort through all of the things we've believed, whether it is from old religious teachings, ghost hunting, etc."

"In your experience, what is the most common message from those on the other side?" I asked.

"There's one thing that's true, one hundred percent of the time in all ADC experiences. I'm talking thousands of them, and that is that the deceased individual [who is] communicating is never sorry that he or she is dead. They seem to prefer it. We the living are stuck in these bags of protoplasm that we have to feed, maintain, etc. The dead are free of that. They're content."

"In reading about all of the positive messages from the deceased during your ADC cases, I was admittedly taken aback when I came across the experiences with those individuals who had committed suicide," I said. "So many people have it burned into their minds that when someone's life ends in that way, they are sent to Hell and are unable to communicate with you."

"Right," he replied. "Which is not true, of course."

Some of the most profound statements in Dr. Botkin's book specifically address suicide:

"The result is deep remorse in every IADC on the part of the person who committed suicide, with the common message being: 'I'm really sorry. I really didn't know my suicide would have this effect on everyone. It wasn't your fault.'"

"Perhaps the most frequent message in IADC experiences is that no one 'gets away' with anything, and that the suffering we cause in other people must at some point be addressed. If IADCs are real spiritual events, then people who commit suicide are not only still left with the same interpersonal issues they were trying to avoid, they also have to confront the additional issue of the pain that their suicide caused in others."

So while it is universally true that the deceased are at peace with being on the other side (at least as far as the IADC patients reported) those who commit suicide are still burdened with the awareness of the sorrow their deaths caused in those they left behind. While Dr. Botkin and I did not spend a lot of time on this particular topic, it was one that had already profoundly affected my life, and one I was initially hesitant to discuss in this book. It is my hope that as you read on, you will understand why I felt it important to include.

As the meeting with Dr. Botkin came to an end, I thanked him for his time, and expressed my interest in possibly working with him on an IADC experience of my own in the future. While I did not have a lingering or debilitating grief associated with the loss of a loved one, the events that had occurred over the past year had certainly brought on a large amount of sadness and discontent that I was finding difficult to manage. He was supportive of my desire to try.

Induced After-Death Communication Therapy with Dr. Graham Maxey

The eleven minutes I'd had with my grandfather in October of 2010 had uplifted and healed me in more ways than I could have imagined possible. The trials I faced in 2011 that brought doubt to the authenticity of that event could not have been more devastating.

Despite all of my attempts to reach him again, I was not able to reconnect with my grandfather through either EVP or ITC. Had I really connected with him in the first place? This was a question that refused to leave my thoughts, and until I was introduced to IADC therapy, I was convinced the answer would likely never come.

When I returned to Dallas, I was admittedly anxious to experience the IADC approach to communicating with the spirit world. I wondered if I could reach my grandfather in that way, and if so, I hoped he'd be able to tell me one way or another if he had been with me during those early morning hours at the Black Swan Inn. Had he been with me on occasions since then that I had not recognized? Would anyone else I loved and missed come through to speak with me?

While I was not suffering grief akin to that of the typical IADC patient, it was a debilitating grief nonetheless, and I wanted out from underneath the weight of it. Part of me remained the diligent researcher, wanting to experience a new avenue of spirit communication and share it with those who'd find it interesting, but in all honesty, I was more motivated by my own desire for resolution than anything else.

In looking through the list of IADC trained therapists in Dr. Botkin's network, I came across a listing for Dr. Graham Maxey in Arlington, just outside of Dallas. He came highly recommended, and I immediately contacted him to schedule an appointment. I explained to Dr. Maxey that while I was perhaps not the typical patient, this therapeutic experience was something I felt would be deeply important to my emotional well-being, as well as to my research. We spent time communicating through email and over the telephone before finally settling on a date for my first session.

IADC Session #1

Upon my arrival to Dr. Maxey's office, I sat down with him to discuss my situation in more detail. I had anticipated a bit of skepticism, though I am not entirely sure why. Had he not believed in the ability to communicate with those on the other side, would he be providing this type of therapy to his patients? I was a bit shocked and relieved when he told me that his wife was a medium, and he most certainly believed that our loved ones were within reach to help and support us. In fact, the two of them often joined forces with their respective talents to heal grief-stricken patients with a great deal of success. I was immediately put at ease.

"You're a bit of an anomaly," he said. "A unique patient, coming from the work you do and the things you've experienced. I can't say I have ever attempted IADC with anyone like you before. This will be interesting for us both."

I knew that IADC therapy had been hugely successful, even with patients who did not believe it was possible to communicate with the dead, but it certainly couldn't hurt that I was already a believer in such things. Perhaps my openness would prove beneficial.

I expressed my desire to see and speak with my late grandfather, and did my best to navigate through the details of the previous year without crumbling into an emotional mess right there in his office. I failed, and miserably at that.

It was not my grandfather's death that I was grieving, rather the idea that my interaction with him since his passing could have been the result of some elaborate hoax. He had, in a way, been given back to me and then doubt had ripped him from my life once again. That second "death" had done far more damage to my emotional psyche than the first.

Dr. Maxey offered me a box of tissues, and patiently listened as I finished telling my story. After I had regained a little composure, he asked if I would be willing to go ahead and attempt the first induction using the bilateral stimulation technique he preferred. He found that administering Eye Movement Desensitization and Reprocessing (EMDR) often left him feeling a bit queasy, but assured me that the same stimulation could be applied by alternately tapping the backs of my hands as they rested on my knees. I closed my eyes, and the induction process began.

I was asked to relax while concentrating on the image of my grandfather. Several minutes passed without incident, and I began to feel myself doubting the process. My "internal chatter" was becoming a problem. I so desperately wanted to see my grandfather's face and hear his voice that my desire became a hindrance. My time with Dr. Maxey quickly came to a close, and I left having little faith that I would be able to make the IADC process work. He assured me that I should not be too terribly disappointed yet, as I still had two sessions in which to attempt it.

On the drive home, I could focus on little else but my failure to remain neutral and without expectation during the session. In the days that followed, I considered canceling my next two appointments with Dr. Maxey. I have never been the type of person to give up on something just because I encountered difficulties, but I had been so emotionally beaten that I wasn't sure I could face any further disappointments. I ultimately chose to return and try again.

IADC Session # 2

When I arrived at Dr. Maxey's office a week later, we briefly spoke about the failure of the first induction. I had done the very thing Dr. Botkin had advised against in his book and in my personal discussions with him, which was placing too much expectation on how the IADC would unfold. If I wanted the second attempt to be successful, I needed to find a way to quiet my mind and just allow it to happen as it was meant to, *if* it was meant to.

I did my best to relax as Dr. Maxey began the induction. I closed my eyes, and simply focused on the darkness in front of me. I asked no questions, and made no remarks. It may have been a matter of seconds, or minutes, but the darkness behind my eyelids began to brighten ever so slightly. My initial thought was that light was simply filtering in from the office window, but as I focused on the brightness, the shape of a person began to form from within it. Everything around me immediately felt lighter, as if gravity were no longer present in the room.

Before I could fully grasp what was happening, I felt the warmth of someone's hands on both sides of my face. And then suddenly, standing there in front of me was my grandmother Marilyn, just as I had seen her before her passing. She looked at me with such a loving expression, and continued to cradle my face in her hands for several moments. The feeling of love and peace I felt in that moment standing there with her is nearly as indescribable as it was miraculous. She had held my face in her hands this exact same way the last time I saw her alive. Neither of us spoke, but I felt overwhelmingly loved.

She withdrew her hands from my face, and turned to look at something to my right. As I followed her glance, I saw my grandfather walk up beside her. She smiled at him, smiled at me, and then she just wasn't there anymore. What she wanted me to know, she had communicated well enough in the brief time we had together.

At this point, I don't remember being aware of Dr. Maxey's presence in the room. I was so happy to see my grandfather that I eagerly began asking him questions.

"Why haven't you come back to see me? I have been asking you to for so long."

"I know why you're sad, April. Let it go," he replied.

I wasted no time in asking him questions. I had wanted this, *needed* it, and here was my opportunity to find some resolution.

"Was it you that I spoke to that evening, on the device?"

He did not immediately answer. Several moments passed, and what he said to me was not at all what I had expected to hear.

"It is okay to love and trust people, April, even if they don't deserve it."

This struck me in a profound way, as I had expected a simple 'yes' or 'no.' He did not elaborate, but I believed I knew the message he was trying to convey. I told him that I loved and missed him very much, took a few deep breaths, and the experience was over. I opened my eyes feeling relaxed and completely content. Two people I loved had come through for me when I needed them to the most, and I couldn't have been more grateful for it. I discussed what I had seen and felt with Dr. Maxey, who listened to the details of my experience with compassion. A few more tears escaped my eyes before I left his office that afternoon, but they were tears of joy, not of sorrow.

IADC Session # 3

When I arrived at his office for my third session, Dr. Maxey had some interesting news to share. His wife had received a message from a man on the other side saying he wished to speak to me. As a therapist, Dr. Maxey is bound by doctor-patient confidentiality and did not discuss details about me with his wife. All she knew was that he would be meeting with a patient for IADC therapy the next morning, and the message was for that particular patient. Prior to my first successful IADC, I had focused all of my energy into speaking with my grandfather. The appearance of my grandmother had been a complete surprise. Did my grandfather have something more to say? Who else would be trying to reach me? I honestly had no idea, but I was certainly ready and willing try it a third time.

I closed my eyes and relaxed once again as Dr. Maxey began another induction. Within what seemed like seconds, I saw my grandmother and grandfather appear again. This time a man was standing next to them with a smile I instantly recognized. I had never seen these three individuals together in life, but it made sense to me that they would appear together now. They were all people I'd loved and cared about. The man standing with my grandparents was Anthony, one of my father's best friends. Had it not been for his signature smile, I would not have recognized him. In life, Anthony had been bald and fairly heavy-set, but as I saw him now, he was quite thin and had a head full of hair.

Anthony had passed away several months earlier, by his own hand. His suicide was a devastating blow, not only to my father, but to everyone who knew and loved him. I had learned very little about the details surrounding the day he passed, as it was not something I felt comfortable asking about. I knew that Anthony had been enduring a number of personal and professional hardships over the past several years; things that anyone would find hard to face.

As I understood the situation, Anthony had made the decision to end his life one afternoon after getting into his car in the parking lot of a business. For reasons known only to him, he shot himself in the abdomen with a pistol he kept in the car. I was told he had made a call to 911 immediately following the shooting. I had wondered if Anthony had regretted the decision to end his life, and had made the call hoping emergency medical personnel could save him before it was too late.

Seeing him standing with my grandparents with that amazing smile of his, I didn't have to ask him if he was all right or if he was happy. It was obvious to me that he was, but I still wanted to know more about the circumstances surrounding his death.

"Did you regret your choice, Anthony?" I asked. "Is that why you called 911 after you did what you did?"

His smile remained, but his expression looked confused.

"No. I didn't regret it," he said.

I told him that his death had utterly crushed my father, and that his family was deeply saddened by his loss.

"I'm sorry I've caused them so much pain," he said. "I didn't intend to."

"How can I help my dad with this, Anthony? He's still suffering with it."

"Just be who you are, April. Just be you."

He wrapped one arm around my grandfather's neck, smiled, and then their images faded from view.

I opened my eyes, and briefly discussed what had occurred with Dr. Maxey. I told him that Anthony had appeared. I explained who he was and what he'd said to me, but that I was more than just a little confused by many of the details of the encounter. Anthony had looked younger and thinner than he had in life, while my grandparents remained older in their appearance. I'd never seen the three of them interact while living, so why were they all together now? How was that even possible, considering the circumstances surrounding Anthony's death? Wouldn't he be somewhere different? Why had he looked confused at my questioning his call to 911? These were all questions Dr. Maxey could not answer, but he was pleased that the IADC process had worked so well for me. He encouraged me to share the experience with my father if I felt comfortable doing so, as he might be able to clear up some of the confusion.

I waited a few days to allow myself some time to fully absorb the things I'd experienced before phoning my father. I wanted him to know that his parents were well and happy, as was his friend Anthony. I knew it would be painful for him to discuss, but I asked him to tell me what transpired the day Anthony died. He told me what he could, much of it I already knew, but when I asked about the phone call to 911 following the gunshot, my father corrected me.

"He didn't call 911 afterward. He called beforehand... to let the authorities know who he was, what he was about to do, and where he could be found."

I spoke to my father about how healthy and happy his friend had looked, hoping it would bring him some measure of comfort. I told him I loved him and ended the call, knowing he probably didn't believe much of what I had told him.

The confused expression I had seen on Anthony's face when I mentioned the 911 call during the IADC made sense to me now. He had not called *after* the gunshot; he'd called *before* pulling the trigger. This fact was unknown to me at the time I had my experiences in Dr. Maxey's office – a fact that further validates the visitation as an authentic one in my mind. He hadn't regretted the choice to end his life, though he did regret the impact it had on the people he loved.

Messages Received

I often revisit the memory of my experiences with IADC, and I am no less affected by them today as I was when they initially occurred. I had walked into them with questions I thought I had a right to ask, and left with answers I didn't even know I needed.

I hadn't asked or expected to see my grandmother, yet there she was. Whether I am recording audio for EVP review, using an ITC device, having a reading done by a trusted psychic medium, or sitting in a therapist's office trying to connect with the other side, my grandmother is usually the first to make her presence known. Her message to me simply being, *I am here.* For me, that is enough.

My grandparents had appeared to me as they looked in the last years of their lives. Anthony was nearly unrecognizable at first. What I learned from this is that spirits are neither defined nor constrained by the physical attributes they had in life. Anthony chose to appear as a younger and healthier version of himself, while my grandparents knew I would appreciate seeing them as I had always seen them.

My grandfather's message, while not directly addressing the validity of the ITC conversation I'd had with him, was simple. I *felt* that he wanted me to let go of my doubts. I *felt* that he had seen and been with me through all of my struggles, and had guided me through them. I *felt* he wanted me to forgive the wrongs that had been done to me and my family, and that he was still very proud of the person I was. I had loved, I had trusted, and I'd been devastated. If people in my life had chosen to abuse my love and trust, it was a weight *they* had to bear; not I. Believing in that conversation was okay, because it brought me peace, and he wanted that for me.

Both my grandfather and Anthony had, in their own way, told me to remain true to who I was. Grandpa wanted me to know I should never regret being good to people, even if they weren't always good to me. Anthony wanted me to hold onto my openness about spiritual matters so that I might bring some measure of comfort to my father over his passing. He had left his life in anguish, but he wasn't lost in some far-off abyss. There was solace in that, and it needed to be shared.

My experiences with IADC brought me the peace I had hoped it would. It showed me that our loved ones truly are ever-present. We may bury their bodies or scatter their ashes, but their spirits are boundless and do not accompany them to the grave. The terms "letting go" and "closure" are just empty words. They mean nothing to someone who has suffered through the death of a loved one. Instead of insisting on figuratively burying our dead, why not keep them close to us?

Love doesn't die when we do.

-11-
Reconciling Research with Religion

"If any of you lack wisdom, let him ask of God, that giveth to all men liberally, and upbraideth not; and it shall be given him."
James 1:5 - The Bible (King James Version)

Becoming a paranormal researcher was not what my family and friends expected of me, nor wanted *for* me. Believe it or not, my initial career goal was to become a corporate attorney. My eventual choice could not have been more of a shock – to me, or to the people in my life. I discovered a love for writing at an early age, and began publishing pieces here and there, never really settling on any one subject or writing style (though poetry was admittedly my first literary love) until I discovered my fascination with this particular work and my underlying desire to write about it. I've always maintained that I did not choose the supernatural; it chose me.

I'd grown up in an LDS household (a member of the Church of Jesus Christ of Latter-Day Saints, or most commonly known as the Mormon faith – not to be confused with the Fundamentalist Church or FLDS) and communicating with the dead was not exactly something the church endorsed. Now, many have and will continue to debate on whether or not Mormons are Christians. There is a whole polytheistic/monotheistic argument (among others) that arises between Mormons and members of different Christian faiths, and it is not an argument I will address here. While I am no longer an active member of the LDS church, I was indeed raised a Christian, and there is no amount of arguing that point that will change my mind.

In the beginning, and as I became more vocal about my interests in the paranormal, my father sat me down to discuss his concerns. He quoted a few scriptural passages, which I listened to and absorbed as best I could. I then proceeded to do exactly as I had always been taught: pray about what was weighing heavy on my heart, and God would surely answer my prayers. The answers I received were not always the answers I expected. I was often confused and disappointed to have received answers completely contradictory to what all of those around me testified was true.

I had been taught about the veil that separated the living from the spirit world all of my life. I knew in my heart it was there. I also grew to know that it was not only possible for me to connect with those on the other side of that veil, but it was certainly not a sin to do so. To clarify, I do not take "counsel" from the dead. They've often voiced their opinions, praised or chided me for various choices, but the only individual that decides the path I will choose to follow is me. My relationship with God is in better condition today living outside of organized religion than it ever was growing up within it. That is just my experience. I completely support the decisions of others to follow their own individual paths, regardless of our differences in religious faith.

I often meet and discuss my work in spirit communication with many Christians who are genuinely curious about what it is I do, and whether or not God approves of it. We are so often taught to let go when someone we love passes away. It is expected of us to live out the remainder of our own lives without them, as if burying them or scattering their ashes will somehow provide us with "closure" until the day we are all reunited. Personally, the process of letting go has provided me with nothing more than a great deal of sorrow. I can't imagine that is what God wants for me, or for anyone else.

In previous chapters, you have learned a great deal of personal information about me. Some might say that on the surface, the work I have done is seemingly positive but that "the devil is in the details." I assure you, in the details that make up my own personal story, the devil is nowhere to be found.

In the interest of presenting two sides to this story, I have asked my dear friend and non-denominational Christian pastor, David C. Cowan, to weigh in with his personal and professional thoughts with regard to paranormal phenomena in general and spirit communication in particular. While he and I agree on many points, we disagree on others. It is our ability to discuss and respect our differing opinions that brings us closer together rather than driving us apart. It is my hope—and ultimately my intention— to encourage a more open and respectful dialogue between those who find themselves firmly planted on either side of the paranormal fence.

Christianity & The Paranormal: Contributed by David C. Cowan

David C. Cowan

First, let me say that I'm very grateful that April Slaughter has asked me to contribute my thoughts concerning the Christian view of paranormal activity. When April asked me to write this portion of her book, I struggled with what to say and how to say it. This was mainly because the topic is so big. Just what do Christians believe about the paranormal? A great many things! At many points in this process I found myself wanting to get very detailed. For instance, even within the Christian community there are various takes on the subject. If one were to ask this question to a Catholic priest, or a pastor in an Assemblies of God church, or a Southern Baptist, or a Mennonite, the responses would be vastly different. What I discovered as I began writing was a labyrinth of information from the scriptures and a thousand ways to tackle this topic. So instead of a lengthy explanation of the Christian view of the paranormal, I thought it would be best to keep the details to a minimum and express what I believe to be the main points of the question at hand.

First, a little about myself. My name is David Cowan. I knew at a young age that God was calling me to serve Him. I was led to follow Jesus by my grandmother. I was baptized in a Southern Baptist church when I was nine years old, and I gave my first sermon when I was sixteen. I married my high school sweetheart after college in Oklahoma, and we moved to New Orleans, where I studied at New Orleans Baptist Theological Seminary. While living in New Orleans, I felt moved to start churches. We moved to Baltimore, Maryland, and started two churches there that met in movie theaters. From there, we moved to Phoenix, Arizona, to do the same. I currently serve as the arts and media pastor at a church in Las Vegas, Nevada.

So why be part of a book like this? I love the heart of a seeker, and I believe God does, too. Anyone in pursuit of truth is a friend of mine. That makes you my friend, because I believe anyone who is genuinely curious about life after our experience here on Earth is a truth seeker. I, too, was a truth seeker at an early age. I was born in Arkansas in 1972 to parents with completely different worldviews. I would describe my father as a postmodern and existential follower of New Age philosophy. My mother, on the other hand, is a conservative evangelical Christian. Needless to say, their marriage did not last.

I felt the weight of my parents' differences as I grew older and tried to discover my own perspective about the world. My time with mom was very structured and organized. Homework after school and church every Sunday were a regular part of life. The time I spent with my dad was almost the complete opposite. I would usually spend my summers with him. My time with my dad was very unstructured and free. Of course, there was no homework, and church was not a priority, but dad was spiritual; he was just more inclined towards New Age philosophy or the occult.

One summer, when I was about fourteen, the difference between my parents' spiritual perspectives became strikingly apparent. My father at that time was very much into the occult. He told me that he was upset that my mother had raised me with conservative evangelical principles, and he wanted me to understand more about what he believed. So he insisted that I go with him to a channeling service. To this day, that stands out as one of the most bizarre experiences in my life. I saw roughly twenty people kneel one by one before a twenty-something woman whose body had purportedly been taken over by the spirit of Saint Germain, a legendary spiritual master of ancient wisdom. The other people in the room would then ask questions of this spirit, housed in the woman's body. In other words, this was not Sunday school with mom.

The differing spiritual perspectives of my parents kept my feet in two unique worlds. Growing up, that was my life. Perhaps this is why April and I are friends and are able to speak cordially while disagreeing about things. She, too, had a foot in two worlds, spiritually speaking, as she expressed in this book. Life in these two worlds has led me to believe there are certain aspects on which both Christians and those in the paranormal field agree. For instance, both believe in life after death. That may seem like a given, but in reality it is not. A growing number of people have been abandoning the idea that we are more than mere leftover remnants of supernovas, that we are merely living creatures, and that when we breathe our last breath, that's it. In contrast to this belief, Christians and others who are passionate about knowing more about what happens to us after we die believe that the journey does not end when our bodies do. This life on Earth is not the full or complete story. Both groups believe there truly is something more to life than just a physical existence. As Yoda said, in *The Empire Strikes Back*, "Luminous beings are we, not this crude matter." I think it's clear that we all agree that something exists beyond this life when we die.

I also believe that both groups are on a genuine search for truth. Both groups really want to know more about this life as well as the life that comes after death. Both seek to understand not only the meaning of life and why we're here, but also our purpose in life individually or collectively as the human race. Much like my experience with my parents, where we differ is in our conclusions.

So, just what does the Bible have to say about the paranormal?

For many Christians, the paranormal is a very difficult topic to unravel. For some in the church, anything paranormal is evil and is not to be messed with. But, to be fair, being a follower of Christ means believing in elements of the paranormal. The Bible is filled to the brim with accounts of paranormal activity: visitations from angels, theophanies, the nephilim, demon possession, miraculous healing, visions of the future, and bodily resurrection from the dead all appear in its pages. Believing in God, angels, demons, and life after death means believing in things outside of the "natural" world. To be a Christian is to believe in the paranormal. Understanding this is crucial. It is not every day that one witnesses a miracle, meets an angel, or sees someone raised from the dead, but each of these things are vitally important to the core of Christian belief because these things are recorded in scripture. I do not assume everyone reading April's book is familiar with what the Bible has to say about these things, so I will tackle of few of these topics.

A quick side note as I quote scripture:

I realize many people struggle with the veracity of scripture. Many people wrestle with believing scripture is true because, in their perspective, the Bible is full of errors and variants, and because of this it cannot be fully trusted. I mean, how can you trust the translators? And what about all of those "hidden" gospels like the Gospel of Thomas? Why were certain books left out? Perhaps this line of thinking describes you. Well, suffice it to say, I know I will not convince anyone otherwise with a paragraph or two here. I probably couldn't convince you over coffee, either, and that's too bad because I love coffee. But what I can do is share a bit about my credentials. I have a Master's Degree in Greek and Hebrew. While working on this degree I was a part of The International Greek New Testament Project (http://www.igntp.org) in which we compared a fifth century manuscript of the Gospel of John written with the Textus Receptus, which is the source from which the King James Version of the Bible was translated. Together with classes in syntax and textual criticism, I have come to understand why there are variants in the text, why certain books were not included, and why the Bible we have today can be trusted. I also understand that flashing my credentials cannot convince you, either. But what I do want to convey is that I am not just regurgitating thoughts from Wikipedia, a google search, or the latest show from The History Channel. Instead, as I have explored my faith, I have determined that the foundation of scripture can be trusted.

Angelic Activity: Messengers/Bearers of Justice/Warriors

From the angels that came to warn Abraham of Sodom and Gomorrah's demise, to the angels that heralded the birth of Jesus, angels seem to be agents of God that come to bring a message. In fact, that's what the word "angel" means: messenger.

Here are a few examples from the Bible where angels are mentioned:

- Warning of impending doom
    - Warning Abraham of the coming destruction of Sodom and Gomorrah
- Freeing Prisoners
    - Peter, Paul & Silas
- Communicating a message
    - To Philip and Cornelius
    - To disciples about the resurrection
- Announcing the coming of a child of promise
    - To Abraham and Sarah about Isaac
    - To Zechariah and Elizabeth about John the Baptist
    - To Mary and Joseph about Jesus
- Preparations of battle/war
    - To Joshua before Jericho
    - To Gideon before battle with the Midianites
- Bringing judgement/death
    - Herod
    - The Book of Revelation

Interestingly enough, the Book of Hebrews tells us that angels can take on physical form and walk among us without being noticed. Hebrews 13.2 (New International Version) says, "Do not forget to entertain strangers, for by so doing some people have entertained angels without knowing it."

My family has experienced what we believe to be two angelic experiences that are hard to explain. In both cases, what we believe to be angels took on the appearance of a policeman. The first happened when I was a very young boy. My grandfather, who had recently been diagnosed with Alzheimer's disease, had been admitted to a local hospital. At some point during the night, he wandered down the hallway and out of the building. My grandmother was home asleep at the time. She was awakened by the sound of her doorbell ringing. A police car with its lights flashing was parked outside, and a police officer with my grandfather in tow stood on her doorstep. The policeman asked my grandmother if the man was her husband. According to the officer, my grandfather had been wandering the streets of Fort Smith, Arkansas.

Feeling grateful for her husband's safe return, my grandmother called the police station the following morning to get the officer's name so she could thank him again. However, the police had no record of an officer doing anything of the sort or even being in that area at the time. She insisted that a policeman dropped off her husband in the middle of the night. She gave every detail she could recall about the time and the man's appearance, but the people she spoke to insisted there was no record of anyone from their department having been at her home.

A few years later, I was living in California with my mom and needed to travel to Dallas to see my dad. It was my first time flying out of the San Francisco International Airport, which was a good distance from our home in Novato. It didn't take long for us to get lost after missing a turn. Since it was the early eighties, we didn't have cell phones yet. My mom pulled over to the side of the road and turned on the dome light to look at a map. Within seconds of pulling over, we heard a voice come over a loudspeaker. The voice asked, "Can I help you?" Immediately, a policeman appeared beside the driver's side window. Mom told him that we were looking for the way to the airport, and explained that she was thinking of taking a particular route. The policeman warned her not to go that way but to take another route instead. We thanked him and went on our way.

It was only after we drove off that we realized a few things were strange about the encounter. When mom pulled over, there were no other cars around, and definitely no police car. We did not see headlights approach us from behind, nor was there any car behind us as we pulled away. We realized that neither of us had really seen the man's face, but only realized he was a police officer because he was in uniform. The directions he gave us turned out to be perfect.

I suppose that a skeptic could find perfectly natural explanations for both events. Perhaps the officer who brought my grandfather home just didn't report what he had done. And maybe when my mother and I got lost on the way to the airport, we just didn't see the policeman parked on the side of the road. Both explanations are plausible, but unlikely. But then again, a skeptic would say that it was impossible for angels to have helped our family in both cases, because there is no such thing as angels. I beg to differ, and I would suppose I am in like company with the readers of this book. There are some things on which we can agree.

Demonic Activity: Influence/Possession/Exorcism

Along with good, comes evil. Unfortunately, it is evil that gets most of the press these days. One does not have to see many horror movies to know that demons and demonic activity is something that never fails to fascinate. In my opinion, demons get too much press, even among Christians. That last statement may surprise you, but I believe it to be true. However, I also believe that demons are real and active in the world today. Here's what the Bible teaches us about them.

According to the Bible, in Heaven, at some point, Lucifer and one-third of the angels incited a rebellion against God and his angels. The results were devastating for Lucifer and his followers. The Book of Revelation says, "The great dragon was hurled down—that ancient serpent called the devil, or Satan, who leads the whole world astray. He was hurled to the earth, and his angels with him." (Revelation 12:9)
Jesus and his disciples spoke of this event in Luke 10.17-22:
> The seventy-two returned with joy and said, 'Lord, even the demons submit to us in your name.'
> [Jesus] replied, 'I saw Satan fall like lightning from heaven. I have given you authority to trample on snakes and scorpions and to overcome all the power of the enemy; nothing will harm you. However, do not rejoice that the spirits submit to you, but rejoice that your names are written in heaven."
> At that time Jesus, full of joy through the Holy Spirit, said, "I praise you, Father, Lord of heaven and earth, because you have hidden these things from the wise and learned, and revealed them to little children. Yes, Father, for this was your good

pleasure.

All things have been committed to me by my Father. No one knows who the Son is except the Father, and no one knows who the Father is except the Son and those to whom the Son chooses to reveal him."

I find it interesting when you read the New Testament's account of the life of Jesus here on Earth, that there are many stories about evil and demonic appearances. There are many examples of demon possession in the New Testament, for example:
Demons are cast out of two men and into a herd of pigs that drown themselves in a lake - Matthew 8:28-34, Mark 5:2-16, Luke 8:27-38
A demon-possessed son - Matthew 17:14-21, Mark 9:17-25, Luke 39-42
A demon-possessed man in a synagogue - Mark 1:23-27, Luke 4:33-36
Demons cast out of many by Jesus - Mark 1:34
Unclean spirits fall down before Jesus calling him "The Son of God" - Mark 3:11
Demons cast out of many by Jesus - Luke 4:40-41
Many with unclean spirits made well by Philip in Samaria - Acts 8:7
Paul casts out of a slave girl a spirit that predicted the future - Acts 16:16-18
The seven sons of Sceva, who are Jewish exorcists, and a demon-possessed man - Acts 19:13-16

And in true Luciferian fashion, and not to be outdone or upstaged by his minions, the devil himself makes several appearances in scripture. His timing is impeccable, and usually occurs when man is at his weakest, or most prideful.

Temptation of Adam and Eve - Genesis 3
The suffering of Job - Job 1.6-12
Temptation of Jesus - Luke 4.1-13
Several times in Revelation - Rev. 2.10, 12:10, 12.12, 20.2, 20.10

Jesus once said to the spiritual elite of his day, "You belong to your father, the devil, and you want to carry out your father's desire. He was a murderer from the beginning, not holding to the truth, for there is no truth in him. When he lies, he speaks his native language, for he is a liar and the father of lies" (John 8.44). This is an important perspective for a follower of Christ: the devil cannot be trusted, nor does he or his followers speak truth. If there is any truth, it's a half-truth at best (which is usually the worst kind because it hooks you like bait as you wait for the switch). Satan also "masquerades as an angel of light" according to 2 Corinthians 11.14. In other words, he's a poser or imitator of what is good, but deceives along the way.

Another important passage from Jesus about Satan is the following: "The thief comes only to steal and kill and destroy; I have come that they may have life, and have it to the full." - John 10.10. Put all of these together and the contrast is clear: Jesus brings life and the devil brings death. One is the genuine article while the other poses as the real thing like a cover band. But do not be deceived; the devil is good at what he does. His deceptions and imitations are stellar, and many are misled. For instance, when people speak with those whom they believe to be friends or family that have died, who is to say the one speaking from the other side is really that person? Considering how the devil is quite good at deception, I would suggest that many have walked away with an experience they believe to be real but have been deceived. Yet they return again and again because they are thirsty for a connection with those whom they have lost.

Communication with the dead:

And all of this leads me to the topic of communicating with the dead, the main subject of this book. One might ask if such a thing is possible or permissible according to a biblical understanding. Possible? Well, in at least one case in the Bible, the answer is yes. Permissible? No. Concerning whether such a thing is possible, there is a passage of note found in the Old Testament in which the failed King Saul uses a medium from Endor to summon the spirit of the prophet Samuel through a séance (1 Samuel 28). Saul had prayed to God for answers, used Urim and Thummim (casting of lots) to discern God's will and inquired of prophets to no avail. The only option Saul reasoned he had left was to consult a medium, something Saul himself had outlawed in Israel. Now some from the Christian community may not even believe that séances are real or even possible, but the text suggests that the person the medium contacted was indeed Samuel. What the spirit told Saul was not good news:

> Samuel said to Saul, 'Why have you disturbed me by bringing me up?' 'I am in great distress,' Saul said. 'The Philistines are fighting against me, and God has turned away from me. He no longer answers me, either by prophets or by dreams. So I have called on you to tell me what to do.'
> Samuel said, 'Why do you consult me, now that the LORD has turned away from you and become your enemy? The LORD has done what he predicted through

me. The LORD has torn the kingdom out of your hands and given it to one of your neighbors—to David. Because you did not obey the LORD or carry out his fierce wrath against the Amalekites, the LORD has done this to you today. The LORD will hand over both Israel and you to the Philistines, and tomorrow you and your sons will be with me. The LORD will also hand over the army of Israel to the Philistines.' (1 Samuel 28.15-19).

Though this case appears to have been a genuine experience, I submit that scripture forbids such practices. So is it permissible? No. As to why, I would say that for the follower of Christ, spiritual guidance comes through Jesus and the Holy Spirit. "When men tell you to consult mediums and spiritists, who whisper and mutter, should not a people inquire of their God? Why consult the dead on behalf of the living?" - Isaiah 8:19

Jesus as our interpretive lens:

Hebrews 4:14 - "That is why we have a great High Priest who has gone to heaven, Jesus the Son of God. Let us cling to him and never stop trusting him." (NLT)
1 Timothy 2:5 - "For there is only one God and one Mediator who can reconcile God and people. He is the man Christ Jesus."
1 John 3.8b - "The reason the Son of God appeared was to destroy the devil's work."

As a Christian, I view God through the interpretive lens of the life of Jesus. I believe Jesus came to Earth from the other side of the veil, lived here for a time, breathed our air, and walked our soil. He got hungry like us, grew tired like us from, and cried tears like us. He hurt when he was betrayed like us, and as it turns out, he also bled like us.

For me, and for followers of Christ around the world, Jesus is our interpretive lens in how to not only see this world, but also the world to come. Why? Because Jesus said emphatically of himself, "I am not of this world" (John 8.23). This world was not his home, but the Heaven where he came from is where we belong, and it's our definitive home. Jesus came as God's representative and a mediator between God and us in order that we might experience this home. In fact, Jesus said the following to his disciples, just hours before he was betrayed and crucified:

"Do not let your hearts be troubled. Trust in God; trust also in me. In my Father's house are many rooms; if it were not so, I would have told you. I am going there to prepare a place for you. And if I go and prepare a place for you, I will come back and take you to be with me that you also may be where I am. You know the way to the place where I am going." (John 14.1-4).

It also describes that when he goes to Heaven, he's going there to prepare a place for all those who believe in Him. This means the work of Jesus in the afterlife is still ongoing, and our life here impacts our life in the next world. His statement also means the life we live here is merely a preface - or just the beginning - for the full story that's ahead.

If all of this sounds confusing to you, you are not alone. Thomas, one of Jesus' disciples, asked Jesus "Lord, we don't know where you are going, so how can we know the way?" (John 14.5)

To this, Jesus answered:

"I am the way and the truth and the life. No one comes to the Father except through me." John 14.6

With these words Jesus utters something that sounds potentially very offensive, but if Jesus is truly God in the flesh and the definitive revelation of God to humanity, I think his words are worth considering. The only one who could fill the shoes of the Way, the Truth and the Life would have to be the definitive statement of who God is and how we are to relate to him.

I think for the most part, many of us search for the definitive, right? Think about it. Peter Jackson's version of The Lord of The Ring trilogy is the definitive version of Tolkien's epic tale. Why would anyone redo them? I feel the same about Charlie and The Chocolate Factory, as well. When Tim Burton decided to redo my childhood favorite, I was disappointed. Though still good, it wasn't great. Why? Because the definitive edition had already been made. In Jesus, according to the Christian perspective, we have seen the definitive of who God is. In fact, Jesus himself says in the Gospel of John, "If you have seen me, you have seen the Father. I and the Father are one." This is why God said in the Ten Commandments not to create and worship graven images. We would mess it up by making God to be like we wanted Him to be and not who He truly is. God wanted to deliver the genuine article. He wanted to deliver the definitive example of WHO God is. For all of these reasons, the life of Jesus is the lens by which I see the world.

So, what if Jesus is the definitive? So what if he is God in the flesh? How does that impact discussion of the paranormal? Well, I cannot think of anything more paranormal that when God steps into time and space. But specifically, there are a couple of reasons that stand out to me.

Jesus and the veil.

As I write these words on Easter Sunday, I am reminded of how the temple veil was torn in two (Matthew 27:51; Mark 15:38; Luke 23:45). The temple veil was a large, thick, curtain that separated the Holy of Holies from the rest of the temple. The Holy of Holies is where the Holy Spirit of God resided. Only the High Priest was allowed inside, and this only happened once a year on the Day of Atonement, or Yom Kippur. Yet on the day Jesus died, this veil was torn in two. This was more than symbolic.

Jesus came from beyond the veil, and when he came, his actions rendered the temple veil pointless any longer. The Spirit of God is now available to ALL who believe. No longer is God for priests or prophets alone, but for anyone who believes.

Jesus spoke of the coming of the Holy Spirit to His disciples:

John 14.16 - "And I will ask the Father, and he will give you another Counselor to be with you forever..."
John 14.26 - "But the Counselor, the Holy Spirit, whom the Father will send in my name, will teach you all things and will remind you of everything I have said to you."
John 15.26 - "When the Counselor comes, whom I will send to you from the Father, the Spirit of truth who goes out from the Father, he will testify about me."
John 16.7 - "But I tell you the truth: It is for your good that I am going away. Unless I go away, the Counselor will not come to you; but if I go, I will send him to you."

Jesus refers to the Holy Spirit as the "parakletos," or "the one called alongside" - - or counselor. The significance is that God's very spirit is now available as a counselor, available 24 hours a day, for one's whole life. I have experienced the presence and power of the Holy Spirit firsthand. I have experienced His comfort and guidance firsthand. My wish is for everyone to experience this same thing. To know that God bridged time and space to have a relationship with me, endured the cross, tore the temple veil, and sent the Spirit for me has changed my life and helped me through many challenging times.

Some of you have lost loved ones, and the pain was excruciating. What am I saying? You STILL hurt. I know the feeling. I'm old enough now to understand that kind *of loss. I don't know of pain much greater for the human soul than to lose a close loved one. It's like a part of us is torn away with no one to patch the tear. But my comfort is not trying to communicate with them again, but rather to lay my burdens down with the one who came from beyond the veil and returned again. I do not gain peace by speaking with spirits of loved ones but by speaking with the Holy Spirit. That's my comfort. That's my solace, and in this I know I am not alone.*

In Conclusion

David and I have spent many an hour discussing our individual views, and I respect him for his willingness to be a part of this book. He is passionate about his beliefs, which is something I deeply admire. While he has expressed concern for my involvement in the paranormal (not unlike many others in my life) he has refrained from passing personal judgment on me for it. It seems like such a slight thing to be grateful for, but it isn't slight to me. He has listened with compassion, understood where we are divided, and been available to me when questions have arisen. He accepts me, even if he doesn't always agree with me. That is my definition of a Christian.

Religious faith is often enough for many people to accept the afterlife as a reality. However, I am not one of those people. It is in my nature to question everything, to push the boundaries, challenge rules, and to discover the truth for myself. Artist and writer Johann Wolfgang Von Goethe once said, "If God had wanted me otherwise, He would have created me otherwise." And that is exactly how I feel about myself and the path I have chosen to take in this life. Do I consider myself any less of a Christian because I happen to talk to the dead? No. In many ways, I believe my experiences with spirit communication and the hope I've been able to share with people because of them is a blessing in and of itself.

I don't practice black magic. I don't conjure spirits to do my personal bidding. There is no voodoo in anything I do. If the devil and his minions were behind my experiences with the supernatural, would I have walked away from them feeling better about being alive? Would I have been inspired to treat others with more compassion and empathy? The simple answer to these questions is no.

Being granted the gift of free will, if I choose to, I can connect with those on the other side of the veil *and* retain my faith in God. Neither one diminishes the other. They co-exist in my life in a way that strengthens me and inspires me to work hard every day at becoming a better person.

I cannot and would not attempt to persuade anyone to believe exactly as I do. I expect the same courtesy from others, though I do not always receive it. When I am approached by individuals who are struggling with their own faith and their desire to connect with the dead, all I can tell them is that it is a personal choice. I recognize that bad and/or negative things are possible in this sort of research, but they are also possible in all of life's scenarios. Denying oneself the opportunity to witness and be a part of something miraculous doesn't make very much sense to me. Ultimately what you believe in and what you practice is your choice; one you shouldn't allow others to make for you.

-12-
Lessons Learned

"For those who believe, no proof is necessary. For those who
don't believe, no proof is possible."
Stuart Chase

There are no experts in the field of paranormal research. That being said, there are certainly a number of intelligent and trustworthy people who pour their hearts and souls into thoroughly researching and documenting legitimate cases of paranormal phenomena. They do not always agree with one another's individual theories, but what is consistent among those who are genuinely interested in the truth is that they remain open-minded and respectful of the work that is being done by their colleagues. Far too little credit is given to those who have most ardently earned it, and these are the individuals I consider closest to being experts as anyone will ever be. I have been honored and humbled to have worked with a great many of them, as the things I have learned have been absolutely invaluable to me and what it is I hope to accomplish.

Perhaps the single most important lesson I have learned in all my years of research is this: Regardless of what an individual (or group of individuals) believes, there is no conclusive evidence of the existence of supernatural phenomena. In fact, the word "evidence" is grossly misused in the paranormal community.

You can be in the possession of the most amazing piece of video footage, the clearest disembodied voice in an EVP, or a mind-blowing photograph of an apparition, but what you have is not evidence. It is data, and while it may be impressive, it cannot be categorized as evidence of the afterlife. Why? Because evidence in this field is entirely subjective. What is evidence to one person is nothing more than the product of an overactive imagination to another.

Take, for example, the debate on what "orbs" really are. These perfectly circular anomalies appear in both video and still photography and are either regarded as a sign that our dearly departed are among us, or they are nothing more than the reflection of dust particles, flying insects, or moisture in the air captured by our cameras. Yes, orbs can be replicated by blowing a handful of dust into the air and snapping off a few photos, but does that mean every orb photograph should be discredited? No, I don't believe that. Personally, I have not seen an orb—either on film or with the naked eye—that would convince me it had a supernatural origin, but that is just my experience. I cannot, with any degree of certainty, tell another individual that the orb they believe to be the spirit of their deceased grandmother isn't exactly that.

Wherever there is genuine information, you will find an equal if not greater amount of misinformation. Fakery is prevalent in this community. Sadly, it is the fuel that feeds the ever-growing fires of disbelief. I have not been immune to it, as previous chapters of this book have illustrated, but ultimately it has not deterred me. Photoshopped pictures of apparitions are a dime a dozen, but their existence in no way detracts from the relevance of photos I myself have taken in which peculiar anomalies have appeared.

I long ago abandoned the notion that my experiences and the data I've brought forth from them would prove the existence of life after death to anyone other than myself. They have, on occasion, inspired people to keep digging for answers on their own; a great reward in and of itself.

The Paranormal Field vs. the Paranormal Community

I bet you're thinking, *Wait, isn't the field and the community the exact same thing?* In the minds of most they probably are, but they really shouldn't be considered as such. Both share a fascination for the other side, yes, but they are two distinctly separate entities (pun intended) functioning at opposite ends of the supernatural spectrum.

The paranormal community is immense and growing larger every day. Anyone with a website, a bag full of electronic equipment, and a black t-shirt sporting a ghostly logo can call him or herself a paranormal investigator. Take the name of nearly any city and plug it into an internet search engine, along with the words "ghost hunters," and you're likely to be confronted with a seemingly endless list of individuals and groups.

Investigations are conducted, "evidence" of paranormal activity is gathered and uploaded to the world wide web, arguments over its authenticity ensue, and a whole lot of back-biting provides the energy that keeps the community moving right along on that hamster wheel I mentioned earlier in the book. No matter how many people hop onto it, it never really goes anywhere.

Don't get me wrong; the community is a great place to learn the basics and to socialize with others that share the same interests. You can see some amazing places and possibly witness some interesting things, but beyond that, what is really being accomplished? If we're being honest with ourselves, it's fairly obvious that there isn't a whole lot of "work" being done.

The paranormal research field, by contrast, is populated by far fewer people. It is comprised of individuals who have a respect for history, who research, experiment, document, report, collaborate with colleagues, and publish their findings. Their work is just that; work. It is not a weekend hobby or something they pick up one day just to put down the next. Many of these individuals are inadequately recognized for their contributions as their material is often stolen, plagiarized, or manipulated by those who wish to lay claim to it or profit from it in one way or another. This is not to say that there aren't wonderful and dedicated people in the community; there most certainly are. Many of them play an active part in it as well as in the research field. It just isn't as common as you might think.

To further illustrate the division, allow me to use my own research in ITC as an example. A large percentage of people within the paranormal community embrace my theories about spirit communication. However, when someone in the community disagrees with my findings, it is not uncommon for them to attempt to publicly discredit or humiliate me. This is not the case among serious researchers. They are never hesitant to share their skepticism with me, but it is always done with respect and more often than not, a new dialogue occurs that inspires both parties to consider other possibilities. It is a mutually beneficial relationship, whether we agree with one another or not.

It is my sincere hope that as things progress, we will be able to bridge the gap that currently exists between the community and the field, and provide each other with a stronger sense of purpose. Keeping that in mind, I feel it is important that I share with you some of the things I have come to know over the years that have not only helped me to experience more of what the other side has to offer, but to understand and benefit from it as well. These are just my observations, and I will never claim to have all of the answers, but these are the things I wholeheartedly believe.

Personality & Choice

There are two extremely important things I find many people fail to consider when it comes to interacting with the dead. The first is that death does not redefine one's character. On the occasions where I believe I've had the opportunity of interacting with the spirits of people I knew while they were living, I have never encountered a single individual who was not wholly themselves after they had passed on. My grandmother is still her beautifully sweet self. My grandfather is still the concerned family patriarch he always was. Who we are—who we really are—survives.

Now, you might think *well, that's just common sense,* but you'd be surprised at how quickly people forget this when trying to establish contact with a spirit. Remember, they are people, not just mindless ghosts. If so-and-so was an ornery, angry person in life, chances are they are probably still that way. The same can be said for those whose countenances are generally positive and uplifting. Whether you are attempting contact with someone you personally know, or looking to make a random connection in an active location, you should remember to address the dead as you would address the living. Pretty simple concept, right?

So, what about those who've passed early on in life? Parents who've suffered the loss of a child, for example, want to know if the child's spirit remains a child, or if there is a progression in growth. It has been my experience that children do indeed mature in their afterlife environment. I've heard from individuals who died young, but came through as much older and wiser than they were while living. We all progress, if we choose to.

Choice seems to be a debatable topic among those with strong opinions about what happens to us when we die. Are we spirited away to the Heaven or Hell we've been taught exists, or do we have some say in the matter? I don't think anyone can definitively say one way or the other, but I believe that our ability to make choices certainly transcends death.

I have spent most of my life trying to unravel the mystery of the people that frequented the basement in my childhood home, only to come to this conclusion: Those who passed through had chosen to do so, for whatever reason. They were not "stuck" there. They came and went of their own free will. The only mystery remaining for me now about that situation is why they were attracted to the house to begin with. There is nothing in the history of the house or the property on which it sits that would suggest spirits might favor it.

When people are told or believe a particular place is haunted, I think it is fair to say that they assume a ghost is always present there in one form or another, even if it is undetectable at times. It is a popular belief that the spirits of those who died tragically are somehow tied to the environment and unable to move on. Perhaps they've just chosen not to, or maybe they aren't constantly haunting the site at all. Isn't it possible that a particular place is often visited rather than continually haunted? People who've had emotional attachments (both positive and negative) to places, people, and even objects might choose to linger for a while after death, or even repeatedly revisit, but can we really label that as a haunting? I believe it is a choice, and far more common than people realize. Yes, I believe those I love on the other side visit me... but *haunt* me? Not at all.

Crossing Over

Go into the light...

This is a term you are undoubtedly familiar with. What exactly *is* that light? Does everyone see it when they die? Are we attracted to it like an insect is to one of those bug-zappers people hang outside over their patios? Choice plays a big part in this too, doesn't it? If I am correct and we retain our free will, taking directions from someone who is not where you are and has never been where you are going seems more than just a little unrealistic to me.

I find it difficult, if not impossible to believe the dead need the assistance of the living to "cross over." How would we know how and where to guide them when we ourselves have never successfully charted the territory we call the "other side?" When asking a spirit to move on and out of our environment, I truly believe it has more to do with our uneasiness at their presence than any actual need on their part to leave. Wanting the best for someone who has passed on is one thing; assuming we know what that is another thing entirely.

Provocation & Respect

If I had to state one reason why I often avoid watching "reality" paranormal television programming, it would be the complete and utter disrespect for the dead that certain personalities think is entertaining. The louder or more confrontational they are, the scarier they think things will become, which then translates into better ratings. Their bravado is just plain offensive to me, and probably just as offensive to the spirits they are attempting to elicit a reaction from.

When people in the paranormal community see this type of behavior on television, many of them end up emulating it because they think that it's the way things are done. If it works for the guys on TV, it's got to be worth trying, right? Wrong. Just because you see someone on TV standing in the dark, barking commands and expletives into the air, it doesn't mean that you should engage in the same ridiculous behavior. There really is no excuse for it, and it is entirely unnecessary.

If you happen to visit a location, and it isn't as active as you had hoped it would be, chalk it up to timing. These things do not work according to our time schedules. **The spirits of the dead are not among us to entertain us.** Yes, it can be fun to run around dark and creepy places and have an experience with the disincarnate, but assuming the revenants you encounter have simply signed up to play haunted house for the amusement of the living is just plain ignorant. Address them in the same manner you would address your friends and family members, because that's who these spirits are: someone's friend, father, mother, and so on. Be patient and show some respect; you might be surprised at how far it gets you.

Famously Haunted Locations

There are thousands of places all over the globe that market themselves as haunted attractions. Having a resident ghost or two can certainly increase patronage from thrill seekers interested in having a paranormal experience. The claims of some of these locations are quite legitimate, but all of them? Hardly. Some resort to hidden trickery to keep up the illusion, and while it is pretty difficult to determine who is up to what, I always caution people to remain skeptical.

If you visit places like the Stanley Hotel in Estes Park, Colorado, the Queen Mary in Long Beach, California, or Eastern State Penitentiary in

Philadelphia (all locations I have repeatedly been to and truly believe to be paranormally active) remember that thousands of people have walked those same halls before you hoping to catch a glimpse of something ghostly. You may or may not be one of the individuals who actually have that opportunity, but I have a word of advice if you're hoping to increase your own personal odds.

Don't do what everyone else before you has already done. The spirits that have chosen to remain are more likely to interact with you if they're not being asked to repeat behavior already requested of them hundreds of times before. How annoyed would you become if hordes of strangers kept asking you, *What's your name? How long have you been here? Can you knock on the wall three times for "yes" and once for "no?"* After awhile you'd get pretty tired of that too, wouldn't you? At some point, you'd probably just shut down and begin ignoring people. I think it is a fairly safe assumption that the dead often do just that.

Many times, showing a little empathy for the environment you're in, its history, and the people believed to be "haunting" it will prove beneficial, and you'll leave feeling as if you made a genuine connection. Think of questions these spirits might not have been asked before. Be there just to spend time with them, and express your desire to make their acquaintance. If all you're after is a good scare, my advice would be to wait until fall when the Halloween season kicks off, and find yourself a good old-fashioned haunted house attraction to walk through.

Ghosthunting Gadgetry

If anyone is guilty of collecting and using a ridiculous amount of equipment during investigations, it would be me. But, it is because I have spent so much of my own personal time and finances investing in various devices that I feel comfortable saying what I am about to say. The gadgets are fun and occasionally useful, but in all honesty, they're costly and mostly unnecessary. We overburden ourselves with the notion that we need things like a 16-channel DVR system to catch a ghost wherever it happens to wander, or a thermal imaging camera so that if said ghost decides to take a rest on the sofa, we'll see the resulting hot/cold spot show up on the cushion.

Is it interesting when something seemingly unexplainable shows up when using technology to detect it? Yes. Is it fun to rewind and relive that moment over and over again? Absolutely, but think of what you could be missing while trying to make sure your technology is set up and working correctly. I highly doubt the ghost of dear Aunt Betty is standing off in the corner thinking to herself, *I'll just wait to come out and say hello until after the cameras are ready to roll. Is my dress wrinkled? Do I have lipstick on my teeth?*

What happened to the good old-fashioned human experience? When did "catching" a ghost become more important than connecting with someone who is in another place and yet still very present in the here and now? Again, the preoccupation with the desire to document "evidence" costs us valuable time and energy, not to mention quite a bit of money. Some of the most inexpensive and yet effective tools in my arsenal are my flashlight and digital audio recorder. That way, I'm not stumbling over things in the dark, and I leave with a record of the event just in case something interesting does indeed occur. Beyond that, what would I really need? My advice to investigators (as well as to anyone interested in experiencing such things) would be to slow down, simplify, and trust your intuition. It will tell you if what is happening around you is real. *You* are your best tool.

The More You Pay Attention to the Paranormal, the More it Pays Attention to You

I have had the opportunity to experience some pretty incredible things when it comes to this research, and people often ask me what it is I am doing to attract as much activity as I seem to attract. My response is always the same. I possess no particularly unique or special talents, yet it seems I have become quite a magnet for paranormal phenomena. Why is this? It's really quite simple. I'm always paying attention.

The house I currently live in was built on land that was nothing more than a pasture prior to being developed, yet my children and I see and hear strange things on a fairly regular basis. My dogs even react to things that have no obvious explanation. Visitors to my home have also experienced a variety of events, and some of them have left believing my house was indeed haunted. I assure you that it is not.

The dead surround us all. They certainly outnumber the living. We as human beings are so busy, so consumed by our routines and responsibilities that we hardly ever have the chance or even the desire to stop and recognize the signs being given to us that we are not alone. When we do recognize them, we often talk ourselves out of believing such things can occur. I would bet that there have been times in your life when you saw the image of a person out of the corner of your eye and thought, *There really wasn't anyone standing there. It must have just been my imagination.* It can't be proven that you saw a ghost, but it can't be proven that you didn't. Instead of instantly dismissing the event, why not stop for a moment to consider that someone might actually be trying to get your attention.

I believe things happen around me because I am open to them. When I ask for signs from the deceased, I do not place a condition on how I want them to be delivered. People often tell me that they want so desperately to hear from their departed family members and friends, begging them for a sign they're still around, and yet nothing happens. My response to these individuals is that maybe they have indeed been given a sign, just not the one they asked for or expected. It is my belief that if you learn to recognize, acknowledge, and express gratitude for the signs you are given, more of them are likely to occur.

I couldn't begin to count how many investigations I have attended with other investigators where a phenomenon will occur, and within seconds it is labeled as something negative or demonic in nature. Yes, I believe that there are negative influences that are aware of us, and like to cause chaos, but I certainly do not think it is as common as people think it is. If you're recording audio, and you hear something akin to growling upon playback, it doesn't mean you're dealing with a demon. Perhaps what you heard wasn't actually growling at all. Imagine for a moment what it must be like for a spirit to impart sounds on our devices. They don't have vocal chords anymore. We have no idea what obstacles they face in communicating with us, or what their energy has to pass through in order to reach us. Honestly, as often as growling sounds seem to be recorded during paranormal investigations, I tend to believe it is more an issue of someone holding their recorder too close to their empty or upset stomach!

It can be frightening when a spirit manifests in whatever form, but if you can be patient enough to just stick it out past that initial shock, I think you'll find that what you are dealing with is, again, just a person trying to overcome a set of difficulties in order to reach you. Interacting with the physical world must be exhausting to those who are anything *but* physical.

For the past couple of years, I have experienced a wide range of phenomena that I not only believe are legitimate spirit communications, but that I actually welcome and find quite comforting. I've paid a lot of attention to the dead. In turn, they've paid a lot of attention to me. One of the most common experiences I have is the introduction of a third unidentifiable voice that often chimes in at various times during telephone conversations.

"Hey... April... Hey..."

There are times I hear it, and there are times the individual on the opposite end of the line hears it. I laugh whenever someone says to me, "Uh, did you hear that? Who is that other person talking?" All I can say is that I don't know. When I've stopped to address the phantom voice, I either can't decipher the response or I just don't receive one. It happens while I'm on the phone with family members, friends, and even on business calls. It doesn't seem to make a difference if I am on a landline or if I am using my cell phone; the voices come through pretty clearly on both. It will happen fairly consistently for two or three days in a row, and then it won't happen again for weeks.

One particularly interesting experience occurred one afternoon while I was busy cleaning my office. I'd disconnected all of the electronics on my desk to make them easier to remove and reorganize. As I began dusting off my desk, the external speakers I usually have hooked up to my laptop started buzzing. I didn't think much of it at first, but after a moment or two, it sounded as if someone were speaking. The external power was still hooked up to the speakers, but they weren't connected to the laptop. I sat in my office chair and said, "Hello? Is somebody there?"

"Hello," was the immediate response.

I called Allen (my husband at the time) into the room and repeated the question, "Hello? Is somebody there?"

"Yes," came clearly through the speakers.

A female voice faded in and out for several minutes, but neither of us could really decipher exactly what was being said. Then it occurred to me that Allen had lost a member of his family to cancer not more than a week or two prior.

I asked, "Is this Sandra?"

"Yes! Yes!" replied the voice.

Sandra was a huge supporter of mine, and had often engaged me in conversation about the research I was conducting. She found it fascinating, and even joked with me a time or two that when she passed, she'd do her best to come by and say hello. Both Allen and I were convinced that she had indeed done just that. Nothing like this incident has occurred on my computer speakers since that day. It may or may not have been Sandra. It may not have been anything supernatural at all, but was there any harm in believing it might have been?

Just For You

For years, I carried my digital audio recorder with me almost constantly. I was so intrigued with my success at capturing EVP that I didn't want to miss an opportunity to record something significant. I'd recorded messages in the daytime as well as the night, in "haunted" locations as well as those that were neutral. I had never believed the dead were only interested in talking to/scaring the living at 3:00 a.m. (aka the "witching hour") as much as the media enjoys perpetuating that idea.

Whenever I sat down to work with the various ghost box devices in my collection, I'd make sure to record the session with both audio and video equipment as well. Not only did this catalogue of data grow too large for me to adequately review, I began noticing a decline in the communications I was receiving during the process. I began to worry that perhaps I was doing something wrong, or that the spirits who had once been eager to talk had grown bored with me and decided it was time to find someone else to connect with.

One evening, as I laid in bed with the inductive amplifier and digital audio recorder rolling, I said, "Is there anything I can do to get you to talk to me again?"

"Turn it off," said a whispery voice.

Turn it off? I thought. *If I turn off the amplifier, I won't be able to hear this voice. Maybe they want me to shut off the recorder.*

I stopped and powered down the recorder and asked, "Is that what you meant? Did you want me to turn off the recorder?"

"Yesss," the voice replied.

Thirty minutes must have passed without hearing any further response from the amplifier, when I asked, "Why did you want me to stop recording?"

"Just... for... you," said the voice.

I must have sat asking questions for another hour or so, but I did not hear any further response. I kept thinking that if I had only left the recorder on, I might have captured something I was unable to notice with just my hearing. I began to feel more than just a little frustrated when the thought occurred to me that whoever was talking to me simply didn't want the conversation recorded.

In the days that followed, and as I thought more and more about that message, I realized one very important thing. Perhaps some spirit communications are meant for the person they are being delivered to, and no one else. I thought to myself, *Would I as a living, breathing individual appreciate it if all of my conversations with others were recorded? Would I want every call or encounter documented for someone else to listen to, analyze, and share?* No, I wouldn't, and I don't think the dead are any different.

From then on, I realized that while I would most likely still record a large number of sessions, I would make a point of setting time and my recording equipment aside to receive messages that weren't intended for public consumption. As a result, I have had some beautifully touching conversations that will forever be recorded in my memory, even if nowhere else.

When reaching beyond the veil, and those on the other side reach back, remember... some messages are meant **just for you.**

Knowing When to Hang Up the "Phone"

Talking to the dead sounds fun, and often can be, but despite its obvious lure, it is not an undertaking meant for every individual. Obsession is not only possible, it's common, and it has the potential to devastate lives. People are not only fascinated by their successes with spirit communication, they are often wholly consumed by them, and begin paying attention to little else.

It is not the content of the message, or with whom the message is exchanged that worries me, as again, I know from personal experience that amazing and life-affirming things can and do happen in this research. But, it is when we forget that we are still alive and have responsibilities that require our energy that spending an inordinate amount of time with the dead becomes a problem.

In the beginning, it took all I had to pry myself away from the various devices in my collection and focus on things such as my writing and other responsibilities, but I have always been fortunate enough to have a strong support system of understanding and patient people around to help keep me grounded. And yes, even the dead find it important for us to step back, hang up the "phone" and get back to the business of being alive.

AFTERWORD

In January of 2012, I was asked to present material on my research in ITC at a paranormal conference in Tampa, Florida. While I was initially hesitant to accept the invitation (as I am with most events) I had reached a point in my work where I felt the message I was trying to share was far more important than my reluctance to get up in front of a large audience and speak. I accepted, and made arrangements to attend.

James, the event organizer, was kind enough to pick me up at the airport and take me out to lunch before delivering me to my hotel to settle in. As he and I sat together enjoying our meals, he asked me several questions with regard to the devices I used, which techniques yielded the best results, and what my personal thoughts were on life after death. It was a comfortable conversation, and one I'd had countless times before with others curious about the work I do. But, as the conversation continued, James asked me a question that had only been asked of me two or three times before.

"What do you think happens to people who commit suicide?" he asked.

"Well, I can't say for certain," I replied. "But I don't think it's hellfire and damnation for every individual who makes that choice. Every person is different. Every circumstance is different. I believe they can be happy, that they can still connect with the living, and that they often do."

My answer seemed to satisfy his curiosity, and the conversation moved forward into other topics. My presentation the next day went well, despite a few minor technical issues. James, as well as those in attendance complimented me on my work and I returned home content with the fact that I had done what I'd set out to do. It was my goal then, as it is now, to reach people in a positive way. At the time, I thought I had succeeded in doing that.

The following April, I received disturbing news. Several individuals who had seen me speak in Tampa reached out to inform me that James had passed away. I wasn't initially privy to the details, but when I learned that James had taken his own life, my heart sank. My thoughts immediately turned to that conversation he and I had had over lunch that January. He had asked me to share my thoughts on suicide, and I had answered him as honestly as I could. But, that was of no comfort to me. I began to feel as though I had in some way, even if unintentionally, given him encouragement to move forward with his choice to end his life. It was a crushing emotional weight I had to bear, and it changed how I viewed and discussed the topic of suicide with others.

Initially, I had decided it was in my best interest to exclude the subject of suicide altogether from this book, as I feared that sharing my experiences with those who had ended their own lives might encourage a repeat scenario. Suicide leaves such an immense path of devastation in its wake, and I would never want it assumed that it was a choice I'd support anyone in making. I battled with myself over the quandary for months, but ultimately decided that my story should be shared in its entirety, and both Anthony and James are a part of that story. As the material was being written and finalized, I found that I couldn't simply ignore the experience I'd had with my father's friend Anthony in the IADC session. To deny you, the reader, the details of such a beautiful and hope-filled experience would have been an injustice to him and the message that he shared with me. Wherever James and Anthony are at this moment, I truly hope they have found some measure of happiness and peace. While the situation was admittedly difficult for me to get past, I know they'd both want me to move forward and persevere, and that is what I've done.

In June of 2012, I returned for my second appearance as a presenter at the Haunted America Midwest Conference in Decatur, Illinois. As with the previous year, I allowed the audience to hear a majority of the ITC conversation I had recorded of my grandfather, but I also had the opportunity to share my experience with IADC as well. Many individuals approached me afterward in tears, and while I had certainly not intended to make anyone cry, it did my heart a world of good to know that I had indeed reached them on a personal level with my story.

As I was sitting in the airport waiting to board my flight home, I checked my email messages and discovered a note from my dear friend Steve Mangin who had attended the conference. Unbeknownst to me, he had taken several photographs while I was speaking, and he wanted me to see them. I was the only individual on stage during my presentation. At least, the only living individual. In the photographs he'd attached, there were additional figures that appeared in different areas of the stage behind me. Whoever they were, I was pleased to see them. In one photograph, to my right and at the far edge of the stage behind the gathered curtain, was the faint and yet discernible profile of a familiar face: my grandfather's.

I smiled, tears streaming down my face, as I stood in line among dozens of strangers to board. While it hadn't really crossed my mind before seeing the photographs, it suddenly occurred to me that I shouldn't have been surprised that my grandfather had been there as I shared my story. He was the central figure, after all. Steve had given me such an amazing gift, and yet another confirmation that I was doing the work I was meant to do.

I feel blessed to have experienced so many wonderful things with this research over the years. I have connected with the spirits of people I dearly loved, those I barely knew, and many that I never knew at all. Even still, my views on life and what awaits us after death are exactly that... *my* views. I will never claim to possess all of the answers to the mysteries of the afterlife; nobody could, but if I am able to continually reach people in a way that encourages them to keep their hearts and minds open, I'll consider my efforts a success.

Bibliography & Recommended Reading

Aykroyd, Peter H. – *A History of Ghosts: The True Story of Seances, Mediums, Ghosts, and Ghostbusters*, 2009

Barker, Elsa – *Letters From a Living Dead Man*, 1914

Botkin, Dr. Allan L. & R. Craig Hogan – *Induced After Death Communication: A New Therapy for Healing Grief and Trauma*, 2005

Ebon, Martin (Editor) – *Communicating With The Dead*, 1968

Guiley, Rosemary Ellen & Rick Fisher – *Ouija Gone Wild: Shocking True Stories*, 2012

Noory, George & Rosemary Ellen Guiley – *Talking to the Dead*, 2012

TAPS Paramagazine – Various issues

Taylor, Troy – *Ghosts by Gaslight: The History & Mystery of the Spiritualists & the Ghost Hunters*, 2007

ABOUT THE AUTHOR

April Slaughter is the author of two books and numerous articles on ghosts, hauntings, psychical research and the unexplained. As an active paranormal researcher for nearly twenty years, she has delved into almost every facet of the unknown from spirits and psychic phenomena to UFO's, Cryptozoology and more. She is one of America's leading researchers into the study of Electronic Voice Phenomenon (EVP), Instrumental Transcommunication (ITC), and is the first to introduce her personal experiences with Induced After Death Communication (IADC) to the paranormal field. She began her journalism career in 2006 writing and working for TAPS Paramagazine - published by the SyFy channel's *Ghost Hunters*. In 2008, she co-founded The Paranormal Source, Inc., a non-profit research and education corporation. April is also the author of the popular traveler's series book *Ghosthunting Texas*, and she continues to write articles for various paranormal publications. When she isn't traveling around the country for research and numerous speaking engagements, she and her twin daughters enjoy a quiet existence among family and friends (both seen and unseen) in Salt Lake City, Utah.

For more information, please visit: www.aprilslaughter.com

CPSIA information can be obtained at www.ICGtesting.com
Printed in the USA
LVOW04s0517160115

423073LV00021B/921/P